Travel phrasebooks collection
«Everything Will Be Okay!»

T&P Books Publishing

PHRASEBOOK

— SPANISH —

I0163380

THE MOST IMPORTANT PHRASES

This phrasebook contains the most important phrases and questions for basic communication Everything you need to survive overseas

By Andrey Taranov

T&P BOOKS

Phrasebook + 1500-word dictionary

English-Spanish phrasebook & concise dictionary

By Andrey Taranov

The collection of "Everything Will Be Okay" travel phrasebooks published by T&P Books is designed for people traveling abroad for tourism and business. The phrasebooks contain what matters most - the essentials for basic communication. This is an indispensable set of phrases to "survive" while abroad.

Another section of the book also provides a small dictionary with more than 1,500 useful words arranged alphabetically. The dictionary includes a lot of gastronomic terms and will be helpful when ordering food at a restaurant or buying groceries at the store.

T&P Books Publishing
www.tpbooks.com

ISBN: 978-1-78492-439-3

This book is also available in E-book formats.
Please visit www.tpbooks.com or the major online bookstores.

FOREWORD

The collection of "Everything Will Be Okay" travel phrasebooks published by T&P Books is designed for people traveling abroad for tourism and business. The phrasebooks contain what matters most - the essentials for basic communication. This is an indispensable set of phrases to "survive" while abroad.

This phrasebook will help you in most cases where you need to ask something, get directions, find out how much something costs, etc. It can also resolve difficult communication situations where gestures just won't help.

This book contains a lot of phrases that have been grouped according to the most relevant topics. A separate section of the book also provides a small dictionary with more than 1,500 important and useful words.

Take "Everything Will Be Okay" phrasebook with you on the road and you'll have an irreplaceable traveling companion who will help you find your way out of any situation and teach you to not fear speaking with foreigners.

TABLE OF CONTENTS

T&P Books Publishing

PRONUNCIATION

Letter	Spanish example	T&P phonetic alphabet	English example
a	grado	[a]	shorter than in ask
e	mermelada	[e]	elm, medal
i	física	[i]	shorter than in feet
o	tomo	[o]	pod, John
u	cubierta	[u]	book
b	baño, volar	[b]	baby, book
β	abeja	[β]	between b and v
d	dicho	[d]	day, doctor
ð	tirada	[ð]	weather, together
f	flauta	[f]	face, food
ʤ	azerbaidzhano	[ʤ]	joke, general
g	gorro	[g]	game, gold
	negro	[ɣ]	between [g] and [h]
j	botella	[j]	yes, New York
k	tabaco	[k]	clock, kiss
l	arqueólogo	[l]	lace, people
l	novela	lʲ	million
m	mosaico	[m]	magic, milk
	confitura	ɱ	nasal [m]
n	camino	[n]	name, normal
ŋ	blanco	[ŋ]	English, ring
p	zapatero	[p]	pencil, private
r	sabroso	[r]	rice, radio
s	asesor	[s]	city, boss
θ	lápiz	[θ]	month, tooth
t	estatua	[t]	tourist, trip
ʧ	lechuza	[ʧ]	church, French
v	Kiev	[v]	very, river
x	dirigir	[x]	as in Scots 'loch'
z	esgrima	[z]	zebra, please
ʃ	sheriff	[ʃ]	machine, shark
w	whisky	[w]	vase, winter

Letter	Spanish example	T&P phonetic alphabet	English example
'	[re'loχ]	'	primary stress
·	[aβre·'ʎatas]	·	interpunct

LIST OF ABBREVIATIONS

English abbreviations

ab.	-	about
adj	-	adjective
adv	-	adverb
anim.	-	animate
as adj	-	attributive noun used as adjective
e.g.	-	for example
etc.	-	et cetera
fam.	-	familiar
fem.	-	feminine
form.	-	formal
inanim.	-	inanimate
masc.	-	masculine
math	-	mathematics
mil.	-	military
n	-	noun
pl	-	plural
pron.	-	pronoun
sb	-	somebody
sing.	-	singular
sth	-	something
v aux	-	auxiliary verb
vi	-	intransitive verb
vi, vt	-	intransitive, transitive verb
vt	-	transitive verb

Spanish abbreviations

adj	-	adjective
adv	-	adverb
f	-	feminine noun
f pl	-	feminine plural
fam.	-	familiar
m	-	masculine noun
m pl	-	masculine plural
m, f	-	masculine, feminine
n	-	neuter

pl	-	plural
v aux	-	auxiliary verb
vi	-	intransitive verb
vi, vt	-	intransitive, transitive verb
vr	-	reflexive verb
vt	-	transitive verb

SPANISH
PHRASEBOOK

This section contains
important phrases that may
come in handy in various
real-life situations.
The phrasebook will help
you ask for directions, clarify
a price, buy tickets, and
order food at a restaurant

T&P Books Publishing

PHRASEBOOK
CONTENTS

T&P Books Publishing

Excuse me, ...	**Perdone, ...** [per'ðone, ...]
Hello.	**Hola.** [ola]
Thank you.	**Gracias.** [graθjas]
Good bye.	**Adiós.** [a'ðjos]
Yes.	**Sí.** [si]
No.	**No.** [no]
I don't know.	**No lo sé.** [no lo 'se]
Where? | Where to? | When?	**¿Dónde? | ¿A dónde? | ¿Cuándo?** [donde? | a 'donde? | ku'ando?]

I need ...	**Necesito ...** [neθe'sito ...]
I want ...	**Quiero ...** [kjero ...]
Do you have ...?	**¿Tiene ...?** [tjene ...?]
Is there a ... here?	**¿Hay ... por aquí?** [aj ... por a'ki?]
May I ...?	**¿Puedo ...?** [pu'eðo ...?]
..., please (polite request)	**..., por favor** [..., por fa'βor]

I'm looking for ...	**Busco ...** [busko ...]
the restroom	**el servicio** [elʲ ser'βiθjo]
an ATM	**un cajero** [un ka'χero]
a pharmacy (drugstore)	**una farmacia** [una far'maθja]
a hospital	**el hospital** [elʲ ospi'talʲ]
the police station	**la comisaría** [lʲa komisa'ria]
the subway	**el metro** [elʲ 'metro]

a taxi

un taxi
[un 'taksi]

the train station

la estación de tren
[lʲa esta'θjon de tren]

My name is ...

Me llamo ...
[me 'jamo ...]

What's your name?

¿Cómo se llama?
[komo se 'jama?]

Could you please help me?

¿Puede ayudarme, por favor?
[pu'eðe aju'ðarme, por fa'βor?]

I've got a problem.

Tengo un problema.
[tengo un pro'βlema]

I don't feel well.

Me encuentro mal.
[me eŋku'entro malʲ]

Call an ambulance!

¡Llame a la ambulancia!
[jame a la ambu'lanθja!]

May I make a call?

¿Puedo llamar, por favor?
[pu'eðo ja'mar, por fa'βor?]

I'm sorry.

Lo siento.
[lo 'sjento]

You're welcome.

De nada.
[ðe 'naða]

I, me

Yo
[jo]

you (inform.)

tú
[tu]

he

él
[elʲ]

she

ella
[eja]

they (masc.)

ellos
[ejos]

they (fem.)

ellas
[ejas]

we

nosotros
[no'sotros]

you (pl)

ustedes | vosotros
[us'teðes | bo'sotros]

you (sg, form.)

usted
[us'teð]

ENTRANCE

ENTRADA
[en'traða]

EXIT

SALIDA
[sa'liða]

OUT OF ORDER

FUERA DE SERVICIO
[fu'era de ser'βiθjo]

CLOSED

CERRADO
[θe'raðo]

OPEN

ABIERTO
[a'βjerto]

FOR WOMEN

PARA SEÑORAS
[para se'njoras]

FOR MEN

PARA CABALLEROS
[para kaβa'jeros]

Questions

Where?	**¿Dónde?** [donde?]
Where to?	**¿A dónde?** [a 'donde?]
Where from?	**¿De dónde?** [de 'donde?]
Why?	**¿Por qué?** [por 'ke?]
For what reason?	**¿Con que razón?** [kon ke ra'θon?]
When?	**¿Cuándo?** [ku'ando?]
How long?	**¿Cuánto tiempo?** [ku'anto 'tjempo?]
At what time?	**¿A qué hora?** [a ke 'ora?]
How much?	**¿Cuánto?** [ku'anto?]
Do you have ...?	**¿Tiene ...?** [tjene ...?]
Where is ...?	**¿Dónde está ...?** [donde es'ta ...?]
What time is it?	**¿Qué hora es?** [ke 'ora es?]
May I make a call?	**¿Puedo llamar, por favor?** [pu'eðo ja'mar, por fa'βor?]
Who's there?	**¿Quién es?** [kjen es?]
Can I smoke here?	**¿Se puede fumar aquí?** [se pu'eðe fu'mar a'ki?]
May I ...?	**¿Puedo ...?** [pu'eðo ...?]

Needs

I'd like ...	**Quisiera ...** [ki'sjera ...]
I don't want ...	**No quiero ...** [no 'kjero ...]
I'm thirsty.	**Tengo sed.** [tengo seð]
I want to sleep.	**Tengo sueño.** [tengo su'enjo]
I want ...	**Quiero ...** [kjero ...]
to wash up	**lavarme** [lʲa'βarme]
to brush my teeth	**cepillarme los dientes** [θepi'jarme los 'djentes]
to rest a while	**descansar un poco** [deskan'sar un 'poko]
to change my clothes	**cambiarme de ropa** [kam'bjarme de 'ropa]
to go back to the hotel	**volver al hotel** [bolʲ'βer alʲ o'telʲ]
to buy ...	**comprar ...** [kom'prar ...]
to go to ...	**ir a ...** [ir a ...]
to visit ...	**visitar ...** [bisi'tar ...]
to meet with ...	**quedar con ...** [ke'ðar kon ...]
to make a call	**hacer una llamada** [a'θer un ja'maða]
I'm tired.	**Estoy cansado /cansada/.** [es'toj kan'saðo /kan'saða/]
We are tired.	**Estamos cansados /cansadas/.** [es'tamos kan'saðos /kan'saðas/]
I'm cold.	**Tengo frío.** [tengo 'frio]
I'm hot.	**Tengo calor.** [tengo ka'lor]
I'm OK.	**Estoy bien.** [es'toj bjen]

I need to make a call.

Tengo que hacer una llamada.
[tengo ke a'θer 'una ja'maða]

I need to go to the restroom.

Necesito ir al servicio.
[neθe'sito ir alʲ ser'βiθjo]

I have to go.

Me tengo que ir.
[me 'tengo ke ir]

I have to go now.

Me tengo que ir ahora.
[me 'tengo ke ir a'ora]

Asking for directions

Excuse me, ...
Perdone, ...
[per'ðone, ...]

Where is ...?
¿Dónde está ...?
[donde es'ta ...?]

Which way is ...?
¿Por dónde está ...?
[por 'donde es'ta ...?]

Could you help me, please?
¿Puede ayudarme, por favor?
[pu'eðe aju'ðarme, por fa'βor?]

I'm looking for ...
Busco ...
[busko ...]

I'm looking for the exit.
Busco la salida.
[busko ˡa sa'liða]

I'm going to ...
Voy a ...
[boj a ...]

Am I going the right way to ...?
¿Voy bien para ...?
[boj 'bjen 'para ...?]

Is it far?
¿Está lejos?
[es'ta 'leχos?]

Can I get there on foot?
¿Puedo llegar a pie?
[pu'eðo je'ɣar a pje?]

Can you show me on the map?
¿Puede mostrarme en el mapa?
[pu'eðe mos'trarme en elˡ 'mapa?]

Show me where we are right now.
Por favor muestreme dónde estamos.
[por fa'βor, mu'estreme 'donde es'tamos]

Here
Aquí
[a'ki]

There
Allí
[a'ji]

This way
Por aquí
[por a'ki]

Turn right.
Gire a la derecha.
[χire a ˡa de'retʃa]

Turn left.
Gire a la izquierda.
[χire a ˡa iθ'kjerða]

first (second, third) turn
la primera (segunda, tercera) calle
[ˡa pri'mera (se'ɣunda, ter'θera) 'kaje]

to the right
a la derecha
[a ˡa de'retʃa]

to the left

a la izquierda
[a lʲa iθ'kjerða]

Go straight ahead.

Siga recto.
[siɣa 'rekto]

Signs

WELCOME!	**¡BIENVENIDO!** [bjembe'niðo!]
ENTRANCE	**ENTRADA** [en'traða]
EXIT	**SALIDA** [sa'liða]
PUSH	**EMPUJAR** [empu'χar]
PULL	**TIRAR** [ti'rar]
OPEN	**ABIERTO** [a'βjerto]
CLOSED	**CERRADO** [θe'raðo]
FOR WOMEN	**PARA SEÑORAS** [para se'njoras]
FOR MEN	**PARA CABALLEROS** [para kaβa'jeros]
GENTLEMEN, GENTS	**CABALLEROS** [kaβa'jeros]
WOMEN	**SEÑORAS** [se'njoras]
DISCOUNTS	**REBAJAS** [re'βaχas]
SALE	**VENTA** [benta]
FREE	**GRATIS** ['gratis]
NEW!	**¡NUEVO!** [nu'eβo!]
ATTENTION!	**ATENCIÓN!** [aten'θjon!]
NO VACANCIES	**COMPLETO** [kom'pleto]
RESERVED	**RESERVADO** [reser'βaðo]
ADMINISTRATION	**ADMINISTRACIÓN** [aðministra'θjon]
STAFF ONLY	**SÓLO PERSONAL AUTORIZADO** [solo perso'nal autori'θaðo]

BEWARE OF THE DOG! **CUIDADO CON EL PERRO**
[kuiˈðaðo kon elʲ ˈpero]

NO SMOKING! **NO FUMAR**
[no fuˈmar]

DO NOT TOUCH! **NO TOCAR**
[no toˈkar]

DANGEROUS **PELIGROSO**
[peliˈɣroso]

DANGER **PELIGRO**
[peˈliɣro]

HIGH VOLTAGE **ALTA TENSIÓN**
[alʲta tenˈθjon]

NO SWIMMING! **PROHIBIDO BAÑARSE**
[proiˈβiðo baˈnjarse]

OUT OF ORDER **FUERA DE SERVICIO**
[fuˈera de serˈβiθjo]

FLAMMABLE **INFLAMABLE**
[imflaˈmaβle]

FORBIDDEN **PROHIBIDO**
[proiˈβiðo]

NO TRESPASSING! **PROHIBIDO EL PASO**
[proiˈβiðo elʲ ˈpaso]

WET PAINT **RECIÉN PINTADO**
[reˈθjen pinˈtaðo]

CLOSED FOR RENOVATIONS **CERRADO POR RENOVACIÓN**
[θeˈraðo por renoβaˈθjon]

WORKS AHEAD **EN OBRAS**
[en ˈoβras]

DETOUR **DESVÍO**
[desˈβio]

Transportation. General phrases

plane	**el avión** [elʲ aˈβjon]
train	**el tren** [elʲ tren]
bus	**el bus** [elʲ bus]
ferry	**el ferry** [elʲ ˈferi]
taxi	**el taxi** [elʲ ˈtaksi]
car	**el coche** [elʲ ˈkotʃe]
schedule	**el horario** [elʲ oˈrarjo]
Where can I see the schedule?	**¿Dónde puedo ver el horario?** [donde puˈeðo ber elʲ oˈrarjo?]
workdays (weekdays)	**días laborables** [dias laβoˈraβles]
weekends	**fines de semana** [fines de seˈmana]
holidays	**días festivos** [dias fesˈtiβos]
DEPARTURE	**SALIDA** [saˈliða]
ARRIVAL	**LLEGADA** [jeˈɣaða]
DELAYED	**RETRASADO** [retraˈsaðo]
CANCELLED	**CANCELADO** [kanθeˈlʲaðo]
next (train, etc.)	**siguiente** [siˈɣjente]
first	**primer** [priˈmer]
last	**último** [ulʲtimo]
When is the next ...?	**¿Cuándo pasa el siguiente ...?** [kuˈando ˈpasa elʲ siˈɣjente ...?]
When is the first ...?	**¿Cuándo pasa el primer ...?** [kuˈando ˈpasa elʲ priˈmer ...?]

When is the last …?

¿Cuándo pasa el último …?
[ku'ando 'pasa elʲ 'ulʲtimo …?]

transfer (change of trains, etc.)

el trasbordo
[elʲ tras'βorðo]

to make a transfer

hacer un trasbordo
[a'θer un tras'βorðo]

Do I need to make a transfer?

¿Tengo que hacer un trasbordo?
[tengo ke a'θer un tras'βorðo?]

Buying tickets

Where can I buy tickets?	**¿Dónde puedo comprar un billete?** [donde pu'eðo komp'rar un bi'jete?]
ticket	**el billete** [elʲ bi'jete]
to buy a ticket	**comprar un billete** [kom'prar un bi'jete]
ticket price	**precio del billete** [preθjo delʲ bi'jete]
Where to?	**¿Para dónde?** [para 'donde?]
To what station?	**¿A qué estación?** [a ke esta'θjon?]
I need ...	**Necesito ...** [neθe'sito ...]
one ticket	**un billete** [un bi'jete]
two tickets	**dos billetes** [dos bi'jetes]
three tickets	**tres billetes** [tres bi'jetes]
one-way	**sólo ida** [solo 'iða]
round-trip	**ida y vuelta** [iða i bu'elʲta]
first class	**en primera** [en pri'mera]
second class	**en segunda** [en se'ɣunda]
today	**hoy** [oj]
tomorrow	**mañana** [ma'njana]
the day after tomorrow	**pasado mañana** [pa'saðo ma'njana]
in the morning	**por la mañana** [por lʲa ma'njana]
in the afternoon	**por la tarde** [por lʲa 'tarðe]
in the evening	**por la noche** [por lʲa 'notʃe]

aisle seat	**asiento de pasillo** [a'sjento de pa'sijo]
window seat	**asiento de ventanilla** [a'sjento de benta'nija]
How much?	**¿Cuánto cuesta?** [ku'anto ku'esta?]
Can I pay by credit card?	**¿Puedo pagar con tarjeta?** [pu'eðo pa'ɣar kon tar'χeta?]

Bus

bus	**el autobús** [el̠ auto'βus]
intercity bus	**el autobús interurbano** [el̠ auto'βus interur'βano]
bus stop	**la parada de autobús** [l̠a pa'raða de auto'βus]
Where's the nearest bus stop?	**¿Dónde está la parada de autobuses más cercana?** [donde es'ta l̠a pa'raða de auto'βuses mas θer'kana?]
number (bus ~, etc.)	**número** [numero]
Which bus do I take to get to ...?	**¿Qué autobús tengo que tomar para ...?** [ke auto'βus 'tengo ke to'mar 'para ...?]
Does this bus go to ...?	**¿Este autobús va a ...?** [este auto'βus 'ba a ...?]
How frequent are the buses?	**¿Cada cuanto pasa el autobús?** [kaða ku'anto 'pasa el̠ auto'βus?]
every 15 minutes	**cada quince minutos** [kaða 'kinθe mi'nutos]
every half hour	**cada media hora** [kaða 'meðja 'ora]
every hour	**cada hora** [kaða 'ora]
several times a day	**varias veces al día** [barjas 'beθes al̠ 'dia]
... times a day	**... veces al día** [... 'beθes al̠ 'dia]
schedule	**el horario** [el̠ o'rarjo]
Where can I see the schedule?	**¿Dónde puedo ver el horario?** [donde pu'eðo ber el̠ o'rarjo?]
When is the next bus?	**¿Cuándo pasa el siguiente autobús?** [ku'ando 'pasa el̠ si'ɣjente auto'βus?]
When is the first bus?	**¿Cuándo pasa el primer autobús?** [ku'ando 'pasa el̠ pri'mer auto'βus?]
When is the last bus?	**¿Cuándo pasa el último autobús?** [ku'ando 'pasa el̠ 'ul̠timo auto'βus?]

stop	**la parada** [lʲa pa'raða]
next stop	**la siguiente parada** [lʲa si'ɣjente pa'raða]
last stop (terminus)	**la última parada** [lʲa 'ulʲtima pa'raða]
Stop here, please.	**Pare aquí, por favor.** [pare a'ki, por fa'βor]
Excuse me, this is my stop.	**Perdone, esta es mi parada.** [per'ðone, 'esta es mi pa'raða]

Train

train	**el tren** [el' tren]
suburban train	**el tren de cercanías** [el' tren de θerka'nias]
long-distance train	**el tren de larga distancia** [el' tren de 'larɣa dis'tanθja]
train station	**la estación de tren** [l'a esta'θjon de tren]
Excuse me, where is the exit to the platform?	**Perdone, ¿dónde está la salida al anden?** [per'ðone, 'donde es'ta l'a sa'liða al' 'anden?]

Does this train go to ...?	**¿Este tren va a ...?** [este tren 'ba a ...?]
next train	**el siguiente tren** [el' si'ɣjente tren]
When is the next train?	**¿Cuándo pasa el siguiente tren?** [ku'ando 'pasa el' si'ɣjente tren?]
Where can I see the schedule?	**¿Dónde puedo ver el horario?** [donde pu'eðo ber el' o'rarjo?]
From which platform?	**¿De qué andén?** [ðe ke an'den?]
When does the train arrive in ...?	**¿Cuándo llega el tren a ...?** [ku'ando 'jeɣa el' tren a ...?]

Please help me.	**Ayudeme, por favor.** [a'juðeme, por fa'βor]
I'm looking for my seat.	**Busco mi asiento.** [busko mi a'sjento]
We're looking for our seats.	**Buscamos nuestros asientos.** [bus'kamos nu'estros a'sjentos]
My seat is taken.	**Mi asiento está ocupado.** [mi a'sjento es'ta oku'paðo]
Our seats are taken.	**Nuestros asientos están ocupados.** [nu'estros a'sjentos es'tan oku'paðos]

I'm sorry but this is my seat.	**Perdone, pero ese es mi asiento.** [per'ðone, 'pero 'ese es mi a'sjento]
Is this seat taken?	**¿Está libre?** [es'ta 'liβre?]
May I sit here?	**¿Puedo sentarme aquí?** [pu'eðo sen'tarme a'ki?]

On the train. Dialogue (No ticket)

Ticket, please.	**Su billete, por favor.** [su bi'jete, por fa'βor]
I don't have a ticket.	**No tengo billete.** [no 'tengo bi'jete]
I lost my ticket.	**He perdido mi billete.** [e per'ðiðo mi bi'jete]
I forgot my ticket at home.	**He olvidado mi billete en casa.** [e olʲβi'ðaðo mi bi'jete en 'kasa]
You can buy a ticket from me.	**Le puedo vender un billete.** [le pu'eðo ben'der un bi'jete]
You will also have to pay a fine.	**También deberá pagar una multa.** [tam'bjen deβe'ra pa'ɣar 'una 'mulʲta]
Okay.	**Vale.** ['bale]
Where are you going?	**¿Adónde va usted?** [a'ðonde ba us'te?]
I'm going to ...	**Voy a ...** [boj a ...]
How much? I don't understand.	**¿Cuánto es? No lo entiendo.** [ku'anto es? no lʲo en'tjendo]
Write it down, please.	**Escríbalo, por favor.** [es'kriβalo, por fa'βor]
Okay. Can I pay with a credit card?	**Vale. ¿Puedo pagar con tarjeta?** [bale. pu'eðo pa'ɣar kon tar'xeta?]
Yes, you can.	**Sí, puede.** [si, pu'eðe]
Here's your receipt.	**Aquí está su recibo.** [a'ki es'ta su re'θiβo]
Sorry about the fine.	**Disculpe por la multa.** [dis'kulʲpe por lʲa 'mulʲta]
That's okay. It was my fault.	**No pasa nada. Fue culpa mía.** [no 'pasa 'naða. 'fue 'kulʲpa 'mia]
Enjoy your trip.	**Disfrute su viaje.** [dis'frute su 'bjaxe]

Taxi

taxi	**taxi** ['taksi]
taxi driver	**taxista** [ta'ksista]
to catch a taxi	**coger un taxi** [ko'χer un 'taksi]
taxi stand	**parada de taxi** [pa'raða de 'taksi]
Where can I get a taxi?	**¿Dónde puedo coger un taxi?** [donde pu'eðo ko'χer un 'taksi?]
to call a taxi	**llamar a un taxi** [ja'mar a un 'taksi]
I need a taxi.	**Necesito un taxi.** [neθe'sito un 'taksi]
Right now.	**Ahora mismo.** [a'ora 'mismo]
What is your address (location)?	**¿Cuál es su dirección?** [ku'alʲ es su direk'θjon?]
My address is ...	**Mi dirección es ...** [mi direk'θjon es ...]
Your destination?	**¿Cuál es el destino?** [ku'alʲ es elʲ des'tino?]
Excuse me, ...	**Perdone, ...** [per'ðone, ...]
Are you available?	**¿Está libre?** [es'ta 'liβre?]
How much is it to get to ...?	**¿Cuánto cuesta ir a ...?** [ku'anto ku'esta ir a ...?]
Do you know where it is?	**¿Sabe usted dónde está?** [saβe us'te 'donde es'ta?]
Airport, please.	**Al aeropuerto, por favor.** [alʲ aeropu'erto, por fa'βor]
Stop here, please.	**Pare aquí, por favor.** [pare a'ki, por fa'βor]
It's not here.	**No es aquí.** [no es a'ki]
This is the wrong address.	**La dirección no es correcta.** [lʲa direk'θjon no es ko'rekta]
Turn left.	**Gire a la izquierda.** [χire a lʲa iθ'kjerða]
Turn right.	**Gire a la derecha.** [χire a lʲa de'retʃa]

How much do I owe you?

¿Cuánto le debo?
[ku'anto le 'deβo?]

I'd like a receipt, please.

¿Me da un recibo, por favor?
[me da un re'θiβo, por fa'βor?]

Keep the change.

Quédese con el cambio.
[keðese kon elʲ 'kambjo]

Would you please wait for me?

Espéreme, por favor.
[es'pereme, por fa'βor]

five minutes

cinco minutos
[θiŋko mi'nutos]

ten minutes

diez minutos
[ðjeθ mi'nutos]

fifteen minutes

quince minutos
[kinθe mi'nutos]

twenty minutes

veinte minutos
[bejnte mi'nutos]

half an hour

media hora
[meðja 'ora]

Hotel

Hello.	**Hola.** [ola]
My name is ...	**Me llamo ...** [me 'jamo ...]
I have a reservation.	**Tengo una reserva.** [tengo 'una re'serβa]
I need ...	**Necesito ...** [neθe'sito ...]
a single room	**una habitación individual** [una aβita'θjon indiβiðu'alⁱ]
a double room	**una habitación doble** [una aβita'θjon 'doβle]
How much is that?	**¿Cuánto cuesta?** [ku'anto ku'esta?]
That's a bit expensive.	**Es un poco caro.** [es um 'poko 'karo]
Do you have anything else?	**¿Tiene alguna más?** [tjene alⁱ'ɣuna mas?]
I'll take it.	**Me quedo.** [me 'keðo]
I'll pay in cash.	**Pagaré en efectivo.** [paɣa're en efek'tiβo]
I've got a problem.	**Tengo un problema.** [tengo un pro'βlema]
My ... is broken.	**Mi ... no funciona.** [mi ... no fuŋk'θjona]
My ... is out of order.	**Mi ... está fuera de servicio.** [mi ... es'ta fu'era de ser'βiθjo]
TV	**televisión** [teleβi'θjon]
air conditioner	**aire acondicionado** [ajre akondiθjo'naðo]
tap	**grifo** [grifo]
shower	**ducha** [dutʃa]
sink	**lavabo** [lⁱa'βaβo]
safe	**caja fuerte** [kaχa fu'erte]

door lock	**cerradura** [θera'ðura]
electrical outlet	**enchufe** [en'ʧufe]
hairdryer	**secador de pelo** [seka'ðor de 'pelo]

I don't have …	**No tengo …** [no 'tengo …]
water	**agua** [aɣua]
light	**luz** [ˡʲuθ]
electricity	**electricidad** [elektriθi'ðað]

Can you give me …?	**¿Me puede dar …?** [me pu'eðe dar …?]
a towel	**una toalla** [una to'aja]
a blanket	**una sábana** [una 'saβana]
slippers	**chanclas** ['ʧaŋklas]
a robe	**un albornoz** [un alˡʲβornoθ]
shampoo	**champú** [ʧam'pu]
soap	**jabón** [χa'βon]

I'd like to change rooms.	**Quisiera cambiar de habitación.** [ki'sjera kam'bjar de aβita'θjon]
I can't find my key.	**No puedo encontrar mi llave.** [no pu'eðo eŋkon'trar mi 'jaβe]
Could you open my room, please?	**Por favor abra mi habitación.** [por fa'βor 'aβra mi aβita'θjon]
Who's there?	**¿Quién es?** [kjen es?]
Come in!	**¡Entre!** [entre!]
Just a minute!	**¡Un momento!** [un mo'mento!]
Not right now, please.	**Ahora no, por favor.** [a'ora no, por fa'βor]

Come to my room, please.	**Venga a mi habitación, por favor.** [benga a mi aβita'θjon, por fa'βor]
I'd like to order food service.	**Quisiera hacer un pedido.** [ki'sjera a'θer un pe'ðiðo]
My room number is …	**Mi número de habitación es …** [min 'numero de aβita'θjon es …]

I'm leaving …

Me voy …
[me boj …]

We're leaving …

Nos vamos …
[nos 'bamos …]

right now

Ahora mismo
[a'ora 'mismo]

this afternoon

esta tarde
[esta 'tarðe]

tonight

esta noche
[esta 'notʃe]

tomorrow

mañana
[ma'njana]

tomorrow morning

mañana por la mañana
[ma'njana por lʲa ma'njana]

tomorrow evening

mañana por la noche
[ma'njana por lʲa 'notʃe]

the day after tomorrow

pasado mañana
[pa'saðo ma'njana]

I'd like to pay.

Quisiera pagar la cuenta.
[ki'sjera pa'ɣar la ku'enta]

Everything was wonderful.

Todo ha estado estupendo.
[toðo a es'taðo estu'pendo]

Where can I get a taxi?

¿Dónde puedo coger un taxi?
[donde pu'eðo ko'χer un 'taksi?]

Would you call a taxi for me, please?

¿Puede llamarme un taxi, por favor?
[pu'eðe ja'marme un 'taksi, por fa'βor?]

Restaurant

Can I look at the menu, please?	**¿Puedo ver el menú, por favor?** [pu'eðo ber elʲ me'nu, por fa'βor?]
Table for one.	**Mesa para uno.** [mesa 'para 'uno]
There are two (three, four) of us.	**Somos dos (tres, cuatro).** [somos dos (tres, ku'atro)]

Smoking	**Para fumadores** [para fuma'ðores]
No smoking	**Para no fumadores** [para no fuma'ðores]
Excuse me! (addressing a waiter)	**¡Por favor!** [por fa'βor!]
menu	**la carta, el menú** [lʲa 'karta, elʲ me'nu]
wine list	**la carta de vinos** [lʲa 'karta de 'binos]
The menu, please.	**La carta, por favor.** [lʲa 'karta, por fa'βor]

Are you ready to order?	**¿Está listo /lista/ para pedir?** [es'ta 'listo /'lista/ 'para pe'ðir?]
What will you have?	**¿Qué quieren pedir?** [ke 'kjeren pe'ðir?]
I'll have ...	**Yo quiero ...** [jo 'kjero ...]

I'm a vegetarian.	**Soy vegetariano /vegetariana/.** [soj beχeta'rjano /beχeta'rjana/]
meat	**carne** [karne]
fish	**pescado** [pes'kaðo]
vegetables	**verduras** [ber'ðuras]
Do you have vegetarian dishes?	**¿Tiene platos para vegetarianos?** [tjene 'platos 'para beχeta'rjanos?]
I don't eat pork.	**No como cerdo.** [no 'komo 'θerðo]
Band-Aid	**Él /Ella/ no come carne.** [elʲ /'eja/ no 'kome 'karne]
I am allergic to ...	**Soy alérgico /alérgica/ a ...** [soj a'lerχiko /a'lerχika/ a ...]

Would you please bring me ...

¿Me puede traer ..., por favor?
[me pu'eðe tra'er, ... por fa'βor?]

salt | pepper | sugar

sal | pimienta | azúcar
[salʲ | pi'mjenta | a'θukar]

coffee | tea | dessert

café | té | postre
[ka'fe | te | 'postre]

water | sparkling | plain

agua | con gas | sin gas
[aɣua | kon gas | sin gas]

a spoon | fork | knife

una cuchara | un tenedor | un cuchillo
[una ku'tʃara | un tene'ðor | un ku'tʃijo]

a plate | napkin

un plato | una servilleta
[un 'plato | una serβi'jeta]

Enjoy your meal!

¡Buen provecho!
[bu'en pro'βetʃo!]

One more, please.

Uno más, por favor.
[uno mas, por fa'βor]

It was very delicious.

Estaba delicioso.
[es'taβa deli'θjoso]

check | change | tip

la cuenta | el cambio | la propina
[lʲa ku'enta | elʲ 'kambio | lʲa pro'pina]

Check, please.
(Could I have the check, please?)

La cuenta, por favor.
[lʲa ku'enta, por fa'βor]

Can I pay by credit card?

¿Puedo pagar con tarjeta?
[pu'eðo pa'ɣar kon tar'xeta?]

I'm sorry, there's a mistake here.

Perdone, aquí hay un error.
[per'ðone, a'ki aj un e'ror]

Shopping

Can I help you?
¿Puedo ayudarle?
[pu'eðo aju'ðarle?]

Do you have ...?
¿Tiene ...?
[tjene ...?]

I'm looking for ...
Busco ...
[busko ...]

I need ...
Necesito ...
[neθe'sito ...]

I'm just looking.
Sólo estoy mirando.
[solo es'toj mi'rando]

We're just looking.
Sólo estamos mirando.
[solo es'tamos mi'rando]

I'll come back later.
Volveré más tarde.
[bolⁱβe're mas 'tarðe]

We'll come back later.
Volveremos más tarde.
[bolⁱβe'remos mas 'tarðe]

discounts | sale
descuentos | oferta
[desku'entos | o'ferta]

Would you please show me ...
Por favor, enséñeme ...
[por fa'βor, en'senjeme ...]

Would you please give me ...
¿Me puede dar ..., por favor?
[me pu'eðe dar, ... por fa'βor?]

Can I try it on?
¿Puedo probarmelo?
[pueðo pro'βarmelo?]

Excuse me, where's the fitting room?
Perdone, ¿dónde están los probadores?
[per'ðone, 'donde es'tan los proβa'ðores?]

Which color would you like?
¿Qué color le gustaría?
[ke ko'lor le gusta'ria?]

size | length
la talla | el largo
[lⁱa 'taja | elⁱ 'lⁱaryo]

How does it fit?
¿Cómo le queda?
[komo le 'keða?]

How much is it?
¿Cuánto cuesta esto?
[ku'anto ku'esta 'esto?]

That's too expensive.
Es muy caro.
[es muj 'karo]

I'll take it.
Me lo llevo.
[me lo 'jeβo]

Excuse me, where do I pay?
Perdone, ¿dónde está la caja?
[per'ðone, 'donde es'ta lⁱa 'kaxa?]

Will you pay in cash or credit card?	**¿Pagará en efectivo o con tarjeta?** [paɣa'ra en efek'tiβo o kon tar'xeta?]
In cash | with credit card	**en efectivo | con tarjeta** [en efek'tiβo | kon tar'xeta]

Do you want the receipt?	**¿Quiere el recibo?** [kjere elʲ re'θiβo?]
Yes, please.	**Sí, por favor.** [si, por fa'βor]
No, it's OK.	**No, gracias.** [no, 'graθjas]
Thank you. Have a nice day!	**Gracias. ¡Que tenga un buen día!** [graθjas. ke 'tenga un bu'en 'dia!]

In town

Excuse me, ...	**Perdone, por favor.** [per'ðone, por fa'βor]
I'm looking for ...	**Busco ...** [busko ...]
the subway	**el metro** [elʲ 'metro]
my hotel	**mi hotel** [mi o'telʲ]
the movie theater	**el cine** [elʲ 'θine]
a taxi stand	**una parada de taxi** [una pa'raða de 'taksi]
an ATM	**un cajero** [un ka'xero]
a foreign exchange office	**una oficina de cambio** [una ofi'θina de 'kambjo]
an internet café	**un cibercafé** [un 'θiβer·ka'fe]
... street	**la calle ...** [lʲa 'kaje ...]
this place	**este lugar** [este lʲu'ɣar]
Do you know where ... is?	**¿Sabe usted dónde está ...?** [saβe us'te 'donde es'ta ...?]
Which street is this?	**¿Cómo se llama esta calle?** [komo se 'jama 'esta 'kalʲe?]
Show me where we are right now.	**Muestreme dónde estamos ahora.** [mu'estreme 'donde es'tamos a'ora]
Can I get there on foot?	**¿Puedo llegar a pie?** [pu'eðo je'ɣar a pje?]
Do you have a map of the city?	**¿Tiene un mapa de la ciudad?** [tjene un 'mapa de lʲa θju'ðað?]
How much is a ticket to get in?	**¿Cuánto cuesta la entrada?** [ku'anto ku'esta lʲa en'traða?]
Can I take pictures here?	**¿Se pueden hacer fotos aquí?** [se pu'eðen a'θer 'fotos a'ki?]
Are you open?	**¿Está abierto?** [es'ta a'βjerto?]

When do you open?

¿A qué hora abren?
[a ke 'ora 'aβren?]

When do you close?

¿A qué hora cierran?
[a ke 'ora 'θjeran?]

Money

money	**dinero** [ði'nero]
cash	**efectivo** [efek'tiβo]
paper money	**billetes** [bi'jetes]
loose change	**monedas** [mo'neðas]
check | change | tip	**la cuenta | el cambio | la propina** [lʲa ku'enta | elʲ 'kambio | lʲa pro'pina]

credit card	**la tarjeta de crédito** [lʲa tar'χeta de 'kreðito]
wallet	**la cartera** [lʲa kar'tera]
to buy	**comprar** [kom'prar]
to pay	**pagar** [pa'ɣar]
fine	**la multa** [lʲa 'mulʲta]
free	**gratis** ['gratis]

Where can I buy ...?	**¿Dónde puedo comprar ...?** [donde pu'eðo kom'prar ...?]
Is the bank open now?	**¿Está el banco abierto ahora?** [es'ta elʲ 'baŋko a'βjerta a'ora?]
When does it open?	**¿A qué hora abre?** [a ke 'ora 'aβre?]
When does it close?	**¿A qué hora cierra?** [a ke 'ora 'θjera?]

How much?	**¿Cuánto cuesta?** [ku'anto ku'esta?]
How much is this?	**¿Cuánto cuesta esto?** [ku'anto ku'esta 'esto?]
That's too expensive.	**Es muy caro.** [es muj 'karo]

Excuse me, where do I pay?	**Perdone, ¿dónde está la caja?** [per'ðone, 'donde es'ta lʲa 'kaχa?]
Check, please.	**La cuenta, por favor.** [lʲa ku'enta, por fa'βor]

Can I pay by credit card?

¿Puedo pagar con tarjeta?
[pu'eðo pa'ɣar kon tar'xeta?]

Is there an ATM here?

¿Hay un cajero por aquí?
[aj un ka'xero por a'ki?]

I'm looking for an ATM.

Busco un cajero automático.
[nese'sito un ka'xero auto'matiko]

I'm looking for a foreign exchange office.

Busco una oficina de cambio.
[busko 'una ofi'θina de 'kambjo]

I'd like to change ...

Quisiera cambiar ...
[ki'sjera kam'bjar ...]

What is the exchange rate?

¿Cuál es el tipo de cambio?
[ku'alʲ es elʲ 'tipo de 'kambjo?]

Do you need my passport?

¿Necesita mi pasaporte?
[neθe'sita mi pasa'porte?]

Time

What time is it?	**¿Qué hora es?** [ke 'ora es?]
When?	**¿Cuándo?** [ku'ando?]
At what time?	**¿A qué hora?** [a ke 'ora?]
now | later | after …	**ahora | luego | después de …** [a'ora | lʲu'eɣo | despu'es de …]
one o'clock	**la una** [lʲa 'una]
one fifteen	**la una y cuarto** [lʲa 'una i ku'arto]
one thirty	**la una y medio** [lʲa 'una i 'meðjo]
one forty-five	**las dos menos cuarto** [lʲa dos 'menos ku'arto]
one | two | three	**una | dos | tres** [una | dos | tres]
four | five | six	**cuatro | cinco | seis** [ku'atro | 'θiŋko | 'seis]
seven | eight | nine	**siete | ocho | nueve** [sjete | 'otʃo | nu'eβe]
ten | eleven | twelve	**diez | once | doce** [djeθ | 'onθe | 'doθe]
in …	**en …** [en …]
five minutes	**cinco minutos** [θiŋko mi'nutos]
ten minutes	**diez minutos** [ðjeθ mi'nutos]
fifteen minutes	**quince minutos** [kinθe mi'nutos]
twenty minutes	**veinte minutos** [bejnte mi'nutos]
half an hour	**media hora** [meðja 'ora]
an hour	**una hora** [una 'ora]

in the morning	**por la mañana** [por l'a ma'njana]
early in the morning	**por la mañana temprano** [por l'a ma'njana tem'prano]
this morning	**esta mañana** [esta ma'njana]
tomorrow morning	**mañana por la mañana** [ma'njana por l'a ma'njana]
in the middle of the day	**al mediodía** [al' meðjo'ðia]
in the afternoon	**por la tarde** [por l'a 'tarðe]
in the evening	**por la noche** [por l'a 'notʃe]
tonight	**esta noche** [esta 'notʃe]
at night	**por la noche** [por l'a 'notʃe]
yesterday	**ayer** [a'jer]
today	**hoy** [oj]
tomorrow	**mañana** [ma'njana]
the day after tomorrow	**pasado mañana** [pa'saðo ma'njana]
What day is it today?	**¿Qué día es hoy?** [ke 'dia es oj?]
It's …	**Es …** [es …]
Monday	**lunes** [l'unes]
Tuesday	**martes** [martes]
Wednesday	**miércoles** [mjerkoles]
Thursday	**jueves** [χu'eβes]
Friday	**viernes** [bjernes]
Saturday	**sábado** [saβaðo]
Sunday	**domingo** [do'mingo]

Greetings. Introductions

Hello.	**Hola.** [ola]
Pleased to meet you.	**Encantado /Encantada/ de conocerle.** [eŋkan'taðo /eŋkan'taða/ de kono'θerle]
Me too.	**Yo también.** [jo tam'bjen]
I'd like you to meet …	**Le presento a …** [le pre'sento a …]
Nice to meet you.	**Encantado /Encantada/.** [eŋkan'taðo /eŋkan'taða/]

How are you?	**¿Cómo está?** [komo es'ta?]
My name is …	**Me llamo …** [me 'jamo …]
His name is …	**Se llama …** [se 'jama …]
Her name is …	**Se llama …** [se 'jama …]
What's your name?	**¿Cómo se llama?** [komo se 'jama?]
What's his name?	**¿Cómo se llama?** [komo se 'jama?]
What's her name?	**¿Cómo se llama?** [komo se 'jama?]
What's your last name?	**¿Cuál es su apellido?** [ku'alʲ es su ape'jiðo?]
You can call me …	**Puede llamarme …** [pu'eðo ja'marme …]
Where are you from?	**¿De dónde es usted?** [de 'donde es us'te?]
I'm from …	**Yo soy de ….** [jo soj de …]
What do you do for a living?	**¿A qué se dedica?** [a ke se de'ðika?]

Who is this?	**¿Quién es?** [kjen es?]
Who is he?	**¿Quién es él?** [kjen es elʲ?]
Who is she?	**¿Quién es ella?** [kjen es 'eja?]
Who are they?	**¿Quiénes son?** [kjenes son?]

This is ...

Este /Esta/ es ...
[este /'esta/ es ...]

my friend (masc.)

mi amigo
[mi a'miɣo]

my friend (fem.)

mi amiga
[mi a'miɣa]

my husband

mi marido
[mi ma'riðo]

my wife

mi mujer
[mi mu'χer]

my father

mi padre
[mi 'paðre]

my mother

mi madre
[mi 'maðre]

my brother

mi hermano
[mi er'mano]

my sister

mi hermana
[mi er'mana]

my son

mi hijo
[mi 'iχo]

my daughter

mi hija
[mi 'iχa]

This is our son.

Este es nuestro hijo.
[este es nu'estro 'iχo]

This is our daughter.

Esta es nuestra hija.
[esta es nu'estra 'iχa]

These are my children.

Estos son mis hijos.
[estos son mis 'iχos]

These are our children.

Estos son nuestros hijos.
[estos son nu'estros 'iχos]

Farewells

Good bye!
¡Adiós!
[a'ðjos!]

Bye! (inform.)
¡Chau!
['tʃau!]

See you tomorrow.
Hasta mañana.
[asta ma'njana]

See you soon.
Hasta pronto.
[asta 'pronto]

See you at seven.
Te veo a las siete.
[te 'beo a las 'sjete]

Have fun!
¡Que se diviertan!
[ke se di'βjertan!]

Talk to you later.
Hablamos más tarde.
[a'βlamos mas 'tarðe]

Have a nice weekend.
Que tengas un buen fin de semana.
[ke 'tengas un bu'en fin de se'mana]

Good night.
Buenas noches.
[bu'enas 'notʃes]

It's time for me to go.
Es hora de irme.
[es 'ora de 'irme]

I have to go.
Tengo que irme.
[tengo ke 'irme]

I will be right back.
Ahora vuelvo.
[a'ora bu'elˈβo]

It's late.
Es tarde.
[es 'tarðe]

I have to get up early.
Tengo que levantarme temprano.
[tengo ke leβan'tarme tem'prano]

I'm leaving tomorrow.
Me voy mañana.
[me boj ma'njana]

We're leaving tomorrow.
Nos vamos mañana.
[nos 'bamos ma'njana]

Have a nice trip!
¡Que tenga un buen viaje!
[ke 'tenga un bu'en 'bjaχe!]

It was nice meeting you.
Ha sido un placer.
[a 'siðo um pla'θer]

It was nice talking to you.
Fue un placer hablar con usted.
[fue un pla'θer a'βlar kon us'te]

Thanks for everything.
Gracias por todo.
[graθjas por 'toðo]

I had a very good time.

Lo he pasado muy bien.
[lo e pa'saðo muj bjen]

We had a very good time.

Lo pasamos muy bien.
[lo pa'samos muj bjen]

It was really great.

Fue genial.
[fue xe'njalʲ]

I'm going to miss you.

Le voy a echar de menos.
[le boj a e'tʃar de 'menos]

We're going to miss you.

Le vamos a echar de menos.
[le 'bamos a e'tʃar de 'menos]

Good luck!

¡Suerte!
[su'erte!]

Say hi to ...

Saludos a ...
[salʲu'ðos a ...]

Foreign language

I don't understand.

No entiendo.
[no en'tjendo]

Write it down, please.

Escríbalo, por favor.
[es'kriβalo, por fa'βor]

Do you speak ...?

¿Habla usted ...?
[aβla us'te ...?]

I speak a little bit of ...

Hablo un poco de ...
[aβlo um 'poko de ...]

English

inglés
[in'gles]

Turkish

turco
[turko]

Arabic

árabe
[araβe]

French

francés
[fran'θes]

German

alemán
[ale'man]

Italian

italiano
[ita'ljano]

Spanish

español
[espa'njol]

Portuguese

portugués
[portu'ɣes]

Chinese

chino
[tʃino]

Japanese

japonés
[xapo'nes]

Can you repeat that, please.

¿Puede repetirlo, por favor?
[pu'eðe repe'tirlo, por fa'βor?]

I understand.

Lo entiendo.
[lo en'tjendo]

I don't understand.

No entiendo.
[no en'tjendo]

Please speak more slowly.

Hable más despacio, por favor.
[aβle mas des'paθjo, por fa'βor]

Is that correct? (Am I saying it right?)

¿Está bien?
[es'ta bjen?]

What is this? (What does this mean?)

¿Qué es esto?
[ke es 'esto?]

Apologies

Excuse me, please.

Perdone, por favor.
[per'ðone, por fa'βor]

I'm sorry.

Lo siento.
[lo 'sjento]

I'm really sorry.

Lo siento mucho.
[lo 'sjento 'mutʃo]

Sorry, it's my fault.

Perdón, fue culpa mía.
[per'ðon, 'fue 'kulˈpa 'mia]

My mistake.

Culpa mía.
[kulˈpa 'mia]

May I ...?

¿Puedo ...?
[pu'eðo ...?]

Do you mind if I ...?

¿Le molesta si ...?
[le mo'lesta si ...?]

It's OK.

¡No hay problema!
[no aj pro'βlema]

It's all right.

Todo está bien.
[toðo es'ta bjen]

Don't worry about it.

No se preocupe.
[no se preo'kupe]

Agreement

Yes.	**Sí.** [si]
Yes, sure.	**Sí, claro.** [si, 'klaro]
OK (Good!)	**Bien.** [bjen]
Very well.	**Muy bien.** [muj bjen]
Certainly!	**¡Claro que sí!** [klaro ke 'si!]
I agree.	**Estoy de acuerdo.** [es'toj de aku'erðo]
That's correct.	**Es verdad.** [es ber'ðað]
That's right.	**Es correcto.** [es ko'rekto]
You're right.	**Tiene razón.** [tjene ra'θon]
I don't mind.	**No me molesta.** [no me mo'lesta]
Absolutely right.	**Es completamente cierto.** [es kompleta'mente 'θjerto]
It's possible.	**Es posible.** [es po'siβle]
That's a good idea.	**Es una buena idea.** [es 'una bu'ena i'ðea]
I can't say no.	**No puedo decir que no.** [no pu'eðo deθ'ir ke no]
I'd be happy to.	**Estaré encantado /encantada/.** [esta're eŋkan'taðo /eŋkan'taða/]
With pleasure.	**Será un placer.** [se'ra un pla'θer]

Refusal. Expressing doubt

No.	**No.** [no]
Certainly not.	**Claro que no.** [klʲaro ke no]
I don't agree.	**No estoy de acuerdo.** [no es'toj de aku'erðo]
I don't think so.	**No lo creo.** [no lo 'kreo]
It's not true.	**No es verdad.** [no es ber'ðað]

You are wrong.	**No tiene razón.** [no 'tjene ra'θon]
I think you are wrong.	**Creo que no tiene razón.** [kreo ke no 'tjene ra'θon]
I'm not sure.	**No estoy seguro /segura/.** [no es'toj se'ɣuro /se'ɣura/]
It's impossible.	**No es posible.** [no es po'siβle]
Nothing of the kind (sort)!	**¡Nada de eso!** [naða de 'eso!]

The exact opposite.	**Justo lo contrario.** [χusto lo kon'trarjo!]
I'm against it.	**Estoy en contra.** [es'toj en 'kontra]
I don't care.	**No me importa.** [no me im'porta]
I have no idea.	**No tengo ni idea.** [no 'tengo ni i'ðea]
I doubt it.	**Dudo que sea así.** [duðo ke 'sea a'si]

Sorry, I can't.	**Lo siento, no puedo.** [lo 'sjento, no pu'eðo]
Sorry, I don't want to.	**Lo siento, no quiero.** [lo 'sjento, no 'kjero]

Thank you, but I don't need this.	**Gracias, pero no lo necesito.** [graθjas, 'pero no lo neθe'sito]
It's getting late.	**Ya es tarde.** [ja es 'tarðe]

I have to get up early.

Tengo que levantarme temprano.
[tengo ke leβan'tarme tem'prano]

I don't feel well.

Me encuentro mal.
[me eŋku'entro malʲ]

Expressing gratitude

Thank you.
Gracias.
[graθjas]

Thank you very much.
Muchas gracias.
[mutʃas 'graθjas]

I really appreciate it.
De verdad lo aprecio.
[ðe ber'ðað lo a'preθjo]

I'm really grateful to you.
Se lo agradezco.
[se lo aɣra'ðeθko]

We are really grateful to you.
Se lo agradecemos.
[se lo aɣraðe'θemos]

Thank you for your time.
Gracias por su tiempo.
[graθjas por su 'tjempo]

Thanks for everything.
Gracias por todo.
[graθjas por 'toðo]

Thank you for ...
Gracias por ...
[graθjas por ...]

your help
su ayuda
[su a'juða]

a nice time
tan agradable momento
[tan aɣra'ðaβle mo'mento]

a wonderful meal
una comida estupenda
[una ko'miða estu'penda]

a pleasant evening
una velada tan agradable
[una be'laða tan aɣra'ðaβle]

a wonderful day
un día maravilloso
[un 'dia maraβi'joso]

an amazing journey
un viaje increíble
[un 'bjaχe iŋkre'iβle]

Don't mention it.
No hay de qué.
[no aj de 'ke]

You are welcome.
De nada.
[ðe 'naða]

Any time.
Siempre a su disposición.
[sjempre a su dispozi'θjon]

My pleasure.
Encantado /Encantada/ de ayudarle.
[eŋkan'taðo /eŋkan'taða/ de aju'ðarle]

Forget it.
No hay de qué.
[no aj de 'ke]

Don't worry about it.
No tiene importancia.
[no 'tjene impor'tanθja]

Congratulations. Best wishes

Congratulations! | ¡Felicidades!
[feliθi'ðaðes!]

Happy birthday! | ¡Feliz Cumpleaños!
[fe'liθ kumple'anjos!]

Merry Christmas! | ¡Feliz Navidad!
[fe'liθ naβi'ðað!]

Happy New Year! | ¡Feliz Año Nuevo!
[fe'liθ 'anjo nu'eβo!]

Happy Easter! | ¡Felices Pascuas!
[fe'liθes 'paskuas!]

Happy Hanukkah! | ¡Feliz Janucá!
[fe'liθ χanu'ka!]

I'd like to propose a toast. | Quiero brindar.
[kjero brin'dar]

Cheers! | ¡Salud!
[sa'lʲuð]

Let's drink to ...! | ¡Brindemos por ...!
[brin'demos por ...!]

To our success! | ¡A nuestro éxito!
[a nu'estro 'eksito!]

To your success! | ¡A su éxito!
[a su 'eksito!]

Good luck! | ¡Suerte!
[su'erte!]

Have a nice day! | ¡Que tenga un buen día!
[ke 'tenga un bu'en 'dia!]

Have a good holiday! | ¡Que tenga unas buenas vacaciones!
[ke 'tengas 'unas bu'enas baka'θjones!]

Have a safe journey! | ¡Que tenga un buen viaje!
[ke 'tenga un bu'en 'bjaχe!]

I hope you get better soon! | ¡Espero que se recupere pronto!
[es'pero ke se reku'pere 'pronto!]

Socializing

Why are you sad?	**¿Por qué está triste?** [por 'ke es'ta 'triste?]
Smile! Cheer up!	**¡Sonría! ¡Anímese!** [son'ria! a'nimese!]
Are you free tonight?	**¿Está libre esta noche?** [es'ta 'liβre 'esta 'notʃe?]
May I offer you a drink?	**¿Puedo ofrecerle algo de beber?** [pu'eðo ofre'θerle 'alʲɣo de be'βer?]
Would you like to dance?	**¿Querría bailar conmigo?** [ker'ia baj'lar kon'miɣo?]
Let's go to the movies.	**Vamos a ir al cine.** [bamos a ir alʲ θ'ine]
May I invite you to ...?	**¿Puedo invitarle a ...?** [pu'eðo imbi'tarle a ...?]
a restaurant	**un restaurante** [un restau'rante]
the movies	**el cine** [elʲ 'θine]
the theater	**el teatro** [elʲ te'atro]
go for a walk	**dar una vuelta** [ðar 'una bu'elʲta]
At what time?	**¿A qué hora?** [a ke 'ora?]
tonight	**esta noche** [esta 'notʃe]
at six	**a las seis** [a las 'seis]
at seven	**a las siete** [a las 'sjete]
at eight	**a las ocho** [a las 'otʃo]
at nine	**a las nueve** [a las nu'eβe]
Do you like it here?	**¿Le gusta este lugar?** [le 'gusta 'este lʲu'ɣar?]
Are you here with someone?	**¿Está aquí con alguien?** [es'ta a'ki kon 'alʲɣjen?]
I'm with my friend.	**Estoy con mi amigo /amiga/.** [es'toj kon mi a'miɣo /a'miɣa/]

I'm with my friends.　　**Estoy con amigos.**
[es'toj kon a'miɣos]

No, I'm alone.　　**No, estoy solo /sola/.**
[no, es'toj 'solo /'sola/]

Do you have a boyfriend?　　**¿Tienes novio?**
[tjenes 'noβjo?]

I have a boyfriend.　　**Tengo novio.**
[tengo 'noβjo]

Do you have a girlfriend?　　**¿Tienes novia?**
[tjenes 'noβja?]

I have a girlfriend.　　**Tengo novia.**
[tengo 'noβja]

Can I see you again?　　**¿Te puedo volver a ver?**
[te pu'eðo bolʲβ'er a ber?]

Can I call you?　　**¿Te puedo llamar?**
[te pu'eðo ja'mar?]

Call me. (Give me a call.)　　**Llámame.**
[jamame]

What's your number?　　**¿Cuál es tu número?**
[ku'alʲ es tu 'numero?]

I miss you.　　**Te echo de menos.**
[te 'etʃo de 'menos]

You have a beautiful name.　　**¡Qué nombre tan bonito!**
[ke 'nombre tan bo'nito]

I love you.　　**Te quiero.**
[te 'kjero]

Will you marry me?　　**¿Te casarías conmigo?**
[te kasa'rias kon'miɣo?]

You're kidding!　　**¡Está de broma!**
[es'ta de 'broma!]

I'm just kidding.　　**Sólo estoy bromeando.**
[solo es'toj brome'ando]

Are you serious?　　**¿En serio?**
[en 'serjo?]

I'm serious.　　**Lo digo en serio.**
[lo 'diɣo en 'serjo]

Really?!　　**¿De verdad?**
[ðe ber'ðað?]

It's unbelievable!　　**¡Es increíble!**
[es iŋkre'iβle!]

I don't believe you.　　**No le creo.**
[no le 'kreo]

I can't.　　**No puedo.**
[no pu'eðo]

I don't know.　　**No lo sé.**
[no lo 'se]

I don't understand you.　　**No le entiendo.**
[no le en'tjendo]

Please go away.

Váyase, por favor.
[bajase, por fa'βor]

Leave me alone!

¡Déjeme en paz!
[ðeχeme en paθ!]

I can't stand him.

Es inaguantable.
[es inaɣuan'taβle]

You are disgusting!

¡Es un asqueroso!
[es un aske'roso!]

I'll call the police!

¡Llamaré a la policía!
[jama're a lʲa poli'sia!]

Sharing impressions. Emotions

I like it.	**Me gusta.** [me 'gusta]
Very nice.	**Muy lindo.** [muj 'lindo]
That's great!	**¡Es genial!** [es xe'njalʲ!]
It's not bad.	**No está mal.** [no es'ta malʲ]
I don't like it.	**No me gusta.** [no me 'gusta]
It's not good.	**No está bien.** [no es'ta bjen]
It's bad.	**Está mal.** [es'ta malʲ]
It's very bad.	**Está muy mal.** [es'ta muj malʲ]
It's disgusting.	**¡Qué asco!** [ke 'asko]
I'm happy.	**Estoy feliz.** [es'toj fe'liθ]
I'm content.	**Estoy contento /contenta/.** [es'toj kon'tento /kon'tenta/]
I'm in love.	**Estoy enamorado /enamorada/.** [es'toj enamo'raðo /enamo'raða/]
I'm calm.	**Estoy tranquilo /tranquila/.** [es'toj traŋ'kilo /traŋ'kila/]
I'm bored.	**Estoy aburrido /aburrida/.** [es'toj aβu'riðo /aβu'riða/]
I'm tired.	**Estoy cansado /cansada/.** [es'toj kan'saðo /kan'saða/]
I'm sad.	**Estoy triste.** [es'toj 'triste]
I'm frightened.	**Estoy asustado /asustada/.** [es'toj asus'taðo /asus'taða/]
I'm angry.	**Estoy enfadado /enfadada/.** [es'toj eɱfa'ðaðo /eɱfa'ðaða/]
I'm worried.	**Estoy preocupado /preocupada/.** [es'toj preoku'paðo /preoku'paða/]
I'm nervous.	**Estoy nervioso /nerviosa/.** [es'toj ner'βjoθo /ner'βjoθa/]

I'm jealous. (envious)

Estoy celoso /celosa/.
[es'toj θe'loθo /θe'loθa/]

I'm surprised.

Estoy sorprendido /sorprendida/.
[es'toj sorpren'diðo /sorpren'diða/]

I'm perplexed.

Estoy perplejo /perpleja/.
[es'toj per'pleχo /per'pleχa/]

Problems. Accidents

I've got a problem.

Tengo un problema.
[tengo un pro'βlema]

We've got a problem.

Tenemos un problema.
[te'nemos un pro'βlema]

I'm lost.

Estoy perdido /perdida/.
[es'toj per'ðiðo /per'ðiða/]

I missed the last bus (train).

Perdi el último autobús (tren).
[perði elⁱ 'ulⁱtimo auto'βus (tren)]

I don't have any money left.

No me queda más dinero.
[no me 'keða mas di'nero]

I've lost my ...

He perdido ...
[e per'ðiðo ...]

Someone stole my ...

Me han robado ...
[me an ro'βaðo ...]

passport

mi pasaporte
[mi pasa'porte]

wallet

mi cartera
[mi kar'tera]

papers

mis papeles
[mis pa'peles]

ticket

mi billete
[mi bi'jete]

money

mi dinero
[mi di'nero]

handbag

mi bolso
[mi 'bolⁱso]

camera

mi cámara
[mi 'kamara]

laptop

mi portátil
[mi por'tatilⁱ]

tablet computer

mi tableta
[mi ta'βleta]

mobile phone

mi teléfono
[mi te'lefono]

Help me!

¡Ayúdeme!
[a'juðeme!]

What's happened?

¿Qué pasó?
[ke pa'so?]

fire

el incendio
[elⁱ in'θendjo]

shooting	**un tiroteo** [un tiro'teo]
murder	**el asesinato** [elʲ asesi'nato]
explosion	**una explosión** [una ekslo'sjon]
fight	**una pelea** [una pe'lea]

Call the police!	**¡Llame a la policía!** [jame a lʲa poli'sia!]
Please hurry up!	**¡Más rápido, por favor!** [mas 'rapiðo, por fa'βor!]
I'm looking for the police station.	**Busco la comisaría.** [busko lʲa komisa'ria]
I need to make a call.	**Tengo que hacer una llamada.** [tengo ke a'θer 'una ja'maða]
May I use your phone?	**¿Puedo usar su teléfono?** [pu'eðo u'sar su te'lefono?]

I've been …	**Me han …** [me an …]
mugged	**asaltado /asaltada/** [asalʲ'taðo /asalʲ'taða/]
robbed	**robado /robada/** [ro'βaðo /ro'βaða/]
raped	**violada** [bio'laða]
attacked (beaten up)	**atacado /atacada/** [ata'kaðo /ata'kaða/]

Are you all right?	**¿Se encuentra bien?** [se eŋku'entra bjen?]
Did you see who it was?	**¿Ha visto quien a sido?** [a 'bisto kjen a 'siðo?]
Would you be able to recognize the person?	**¿Sería capaz de reconocer a la persona?** [se'ria ka'paθ de rekono'θer a lʲa per'sona?]
Are you sure?	**¿Está usted seguro?** [es'ta us'te se'ɣuro?]

Please calm down.	**Por favor, cálmese.** [por fa'βor, 'kalʲmese]
Take it easy!	**¡Cálmese!** [kalʲmese!]
Don't worry!	**¡No se preocupe!** [no se preo'kupe!]
Everything will be fine.	**Todo irá bien.** [toðo i'ra bjen]
Everything's all right.	**Todo está bien.** [toðo es'ta bjen]

Come here, please.

Venga aquí, por favor.
[benga a'ki, por fa'βor]

I have some questions for you.

Tengo unas preguntas para usted.
[tengo 'unas pre'ɣuntas 'para us'te]

Wait a moment, please.

Espere un momento, por favor.
[es'pere un mo'mento, por fa'βor]

Do you have any I.D.?

¿Tiene un documento de identidad?
[tjene un doku'mento de iðenti'ðað?]

Thanks. You can leave now.

Gracias. Puede irse ahora.
[graθjas. pu'eðe 'irse a'ora]

Hands behind your head!

¡Manos detrás de la cabeza!
[manos de'tras de lʲa ka'βeθa!]

You're under arrest!

¡Está arrestado /arrestada/!
[es'ta ares'taðo /ares'taða/!]

Health problems

Please help me.
Ayudeme, por favor.
[a'juðeme, por fa'βor]

I don't feel well.
No me encuentro bien.
[no me eŋku'entro bjen]

My husband doesn't feel well.
Mi marido no se encuentra bien.
[mi ma'riðo no se eŋku'entra bjen]

My son ...
Mi hijo ...
[mi 'iχo ...]

My father ...
Mi padre ...
[mi 'paðre ...]

My wife doesn't feel well.
Mi mujer no se encuentra bien.
[mi mu'χer no se eŋku'entra bjen]

My daughter ...
Mi hija ...
[mi 'iχa ...]

My mother ...
Mi madre ...
[mi 'maðre ...]

I've got a ...
Me duele ...
[me du'ele ...]

headache
la cabeza
[lʲa ka'βeθa]

sore throat
la garganta
[lʲa gar'ɣanta]

stomach ache
el estómago
[elʲ es'tomaɣo]

toothache
un diente
[un 'djente]

I feel dizzy.
Estoy mareado.
[es'toj mare'aðo]

He has a fever.
Él tiene fiebre.
[elʲ 'tjene 'fjeβre]

She has a fever.
Ella tiene fiebre.
[eja 'tjene 'fjeβre]

I can't breathe.
No puedo respirar.
[no pu'eðo respi'rar]

I'm short of breath.
Me ahogo.
[me a'oɣo]

I am asthmatic.
Tengo asma.
[tengo 'asma]

I am diabetic.
Tengo diabetes.
[tengo dja'βetes]

I can't sleep.	**No puedo dormir.** [no pu'eðo dor'mir]
food poisoning	**intoxicación alimentaria** [intoksika'θjon alimen'tarja]

It hurts here.	**Me duele aquí.** [me du'ele a'ki]
Help me!	**¡Ayúdeme!** [a'juðeme!]
I am here!	**¡Estoy aquí!** [es'toj a'ki!]
We are here!	**¡Estamos aquí!** [es'tamos a'ki!]
Get me out of here!	**¡Saquenme de aquí!** [sa'kenme de a'ki!]
I need a doctor.	**Necesito un médico.** [neθe'sito un 'meðiko]
I can't move.	**No me puedo mover.** [no me pu'eðo mo'βer]
I can't move my legs.	**No puedo mover mis piernas.** [no pu'eðo mo'βer mis 'pjernas]

I have a wound.	**Tengo una herida.** [tengo 'una e'riða]
Is it serious?	**¿Es grave?** [es 'graβe?]
My documents are in my pocket.	**Mis documentos están en mi bolsillo.** [mis doku'mentos es'tan en mi bol'sijo]
Calm down!	**¡Cálmese!** [kal'mese!]
May I use your phone?	**¿Puedo usar su teléfono?** [pu'eðo u'sar su te'lefono?]

Call an ambulance!	**¡Llame a la ambulancia!** [jame a la ambu'lanθja!]
It's urgent!	**¡Es urgente!** [es ur'xente!]
It's an emergency!	**¡Es una emergencia!** [es 'una emer'xenθja!]
Please hurry up!	**¡Más rápido, por favor!** [mas 'rapiðo, por fa'βor!]
Would you please call a doctor?	**¿Puede llamar a un médico, por favor?** [pu'eðe ja'mar a un 'meðiko, por fa'βor?]
Where is the hospital?	**¿Dónde está el hospital?** [donde es'ta elʲ ospi'talʲ?]

How are you feeling?	**¿Cómo se siente?** [komo se 'sjente?]
Are you all right?	**¿Se encuentra bien?** [se eŋku'entra bjen?]

What's happened?

¿Qué pasó?
[ke pa'so?]

I feel better now.

Me encuentro mejor.
[me eŋku'entro me'xor]

It's OK.

Está bien.
[es'ta bjen]

It's all right.

Todo está bien.
[toðo es'ta bjen]

At the pharmacy

pharmacy (drugstore)	**la farmacia** [lʲa far'maθja]
24-hour pharmacy	**la farmacia 24 (veinte cuatro) horas** [lʲa far'maθja 'bejnte ku'atro 'oras]
Where is the closest pharmacy?	**¿Dónde está la farmacia más cercana?** [donde es'ta lʲa far'maθja mas θer'kana?]
Is it open now?	**¿Está abierta ahora?** [es'ta a'βjerta a'ora?]
At what time does it open?	**¿A qué hora abre?** [a ke 'ora 'aβre?]
At what time does it close?	**¿A qué hora cierra?** [a ke 'ora 'θjera?]
Is it far?	**¿Está lejos?** [es'ta 'leχos?]
Can I get there on foot?	**¿Puedo llegar a pie?** [pu'eðo je'ɣar a pje?]
Can you show me on the map?	**¿Puede mostrarme en el mapa?** [pu'eðe mos'trarme en elʲ 'mapa?]
Please give me something for ...	**Por favor, deme algo para ...** [por fa'βor, 'deme 'alʲɣo 'para ...]
a headache	**un dolor de cabeza** [un do'lor de ka'βeθa]
a cough	**la tos** [lʲa tos]
a cold	**el resfriado** [elʲ resfri'aðo]
the flu	**la gripe** [lʲa 'gripe]
a fever	**la fiebre** [lʲa 'fjeβre]
a stomach ache	**un dolor de estomago** [un do'lor de es'tomaɣo]
nausea	**nauseas** [nau'seas]
diarrhea	**la diarrea** [lʲa dja'rea]
constipation	**el estreñimiento** [elʲ estrenji'mjento]

pain in the back	**un dolor de espalda** [un do'lor de esˈpalʲda]
chest pain	**un dolor de pecho** [un do'lor de ˈpeʧo]
side stitch	**el flato** [elʲ ˈflato]
abdominal pain	**un dolor abdominal** [un do'lor aβðomiˈnalʲ]

pill	**la píldora** [lʲa ˈpilʲðora]
ointment, cream	**la crema** [lʲa ˈkrema]
syrup	**el jarabe** [elʲ χaˈraβe]
spray	**el spray** [elʲ spraj]
drops	**las gotas** [lʲas ˈgotas]

You need to go to the hospital.	**Tiene que ir al hospital.** [tjene ke ir alʲ ospiˈtalʲ]
health insurance	**el seguro de salud** [se'ɣuro de sa'lʲuð]
prescription	**la receta** [re'θeta]
insect repellant	**el repelente de insectos** [el repeˈlente de inˈsektos]
Band Aid	**la curita** [lʲa kuˈrita]

The bare minimum

Excuse me, ...	**Perdone, ...** [per'ðone, ...]
Hello.	**Hola.** [ola]
Thank you.	**Gracias.** [graθjas]
Good bye.	**Adiós.** [a'ðjos]
Yes.	**Sí.** [si]
No.	**No.** [no]
I don't know.	**No lo sé.** [no lo 'se]
Where?	Where to?	When?	**¿Dónde?	¿A dónde?	¿Cuándo?** [donde?	a 'donde?	ku'ando?]
I need ...	**Necesito ...** [neθe'sito ...]
I want ...	**Quiero ...** [kjero ...]
Do you have ...?	**¿Tiene ...?** [tjene ...?]
Is there a ... here?	**¿Hay ... por aquí?** [aj ... por a'ki?]
May I ...?	**¿Puedo ...?** [pu'eðo ...?]
..., please (polite request)	**..., por favor** [..., por fa'βor]
I'm looking for ...	**Busco ...** [busko ...]
the restroom	**el servicio** [elʲ ser'βiθjo]
an ATM	**un cajero** [un ka'χero]
a pharmacy (drugstore)	**una farmacia** [una far'maθja]
a hospital	**el hospital** [elʲ ospi'talʲ]
the police station	**la comisaría** [lʲa komisa'ria]
the subway	**el metro** [elʲ 'metro]

a taxi	**un taxi** [un 'taksi]
the train station	**la estación de tren** [lʲa esta'θjon de tren]

My name is ...	**Me llamo ...** [me 'jamo ...]
What's your name?	**¿Cómo se llama?** [komo se 'jama?]
Could you please help me?	**¿Puede ayudarme, por favor?** [pu'eðe aju'ðarme, por fa'βor?]
I've got a problem.	**Tengo un problema.** [tengo un pro'βlema]
I don't feel well.	**Me encuentro mal.** [me eŋku'entro malʲ]
Call an ambulance!	**¡Llame a la ambulancia!** [jame a la ambu'lanθja!]
May I make a call?	**¿Puedo llamar, por favor?** [pu'eðo ja'mar, por fa'βor?]

I'm sorry.	**Lo siento.** [lo 'sjento]
You're welcome.	**De nada.** [ðe 'naða]

I, me	**Yo** [jo]
you (inform.)	**tú** [tu]
he	**él** [elʲ]
she	**ella** [eja]
they (masc.)	**ellos** [ejos]
they (fem.)	**ellas** [ejas]
we	**nosotros** [no'sotros]
you (pl)	**ustedes	vosotros** [us'teðes	bo'sotros]
you (sg, form.)	**usted** [us'teð]

ENTRANCE	**ENTRADA** [en'traða]
EXIT	**SALIDA** [sa'liða]
OUT OF ORDER	**FUERA DE SERVICIO** [fu'era de ser'βiθjo]
CLOSED	**CERRADO** [θe'raðo]

OPEN	**ABIERTO** [a'βjerto]
FOR WOMEN	**PARA SEÑORAS** [para se'njoras]
FOR MEN	**PARA CABALLEROS** [para kaβa'jeros]

CONCISE DICTIONARY

This section contains more than 1,500 useful words arranged alphabetically. The dictionary includes a lot of gastronomic terms and will be helpful when ordering food at a restaurant or buying groceries

T&P Books Publishing

DICTIONARY CONTENTS

T&P Books Publishing

1. Time. Calendar

time	**tiempo** (m)	['tjempo]
hour	**hora** (f)	['ora]
half an hour	**media hora** (f)	['meðja 'ora]
minute	**minuto** (m)	[mi'nuto]
second	**segundo** (m)	[se'ɣundo]
today (adv)	**hoy** (adv)	[oj]
tomorrow (adv)	**mañana** (adv)	[ma'njana]
yesterday (adv)	**ayer** (adv)	[a'jer]
Monday	**lunes** (m)	['lʲunes]
Tuesday	**martes** (m)	['martes]
Wednesday	**miércoles** (m)	['mjerkoles]
Thursday	**jueves** (m)	[χu'eβes]
Friday	**viernes** (m)	['bjernes]
Saturday	**sábado** (m)	['saβaðo]
Sunday	**domingo** (m)	[do'mingo]
day	**día** (m)	['dia]
working day	**día** (m) **de trabajo**	['dia de tra'βaχo]
public holiday	**día** (m) **de fiesta**	['dia de 'fjesta]
weekend	**fin** (m) **de semana**	['fin de se'mana]
week	**semana** (f)	[se'mana]
last week (adv)	**semana** (f) **pasada**	[se'mana pa'saða]
next week (adv)	**semana** (f) **que viene**	[se'mana ke 'bjene]
sunrise	**salida** (f) **del sol**	[sa'liða delʲ 'solʲ]
sunset	**puesta** (f) **del sol**	[pu'esta delʲ 'solʲ]
in the morning	**por la mañana**	[por lʲa ma'njana]
in the afternoon	**por la tarde**	[por lʲa 'tarðe]
in the evening	**por la noche**	[por lʲa 'notʃe]
tonight (this evening)	**esta noche**	['esta 'notʃe]
at night	**por la noche**	[por lʲa 'notʃe]
midnight	**medianoche** (f)	['meðja'notʃe]
January	**enero** (m)	[e'nero]
February	**febrero** (m)	[fe'βrero]
March	**marzo** (m)	['marθo]
April	**abril** (m)	[a'βrilʲ]
May	**mayo** (m)	['majo]
June	**junio** (m)	['χunjo]

July	**julio** (m)	['χuljo]
August	**agosto** (m)	[a'ɣosto]
September	**septiembre** (m)	[sep'tjembre]
October	**octubre** (m)	[ok'tuβre]
November	**noviembre** (m)	[no'βjembre]
December	**diciembre** (m)	[di'θjembre]
in spring	**en primavera**	[en prima'βera]
in summer	**en verano**	[em be'rano]
in fall	**en otoño**	[en o'tonjo]
in winter	**en invierno**	[en im'bjerno]
month	**mes** (m)	[mes]
season (summer, etc.)	**estación** (f)	[esta'θjon]
year	**año** (m)	['anjo]
century	**siglo** (m)	['siɣlo]

2. Numbers. Numerals

digit, figure	**cifra** (f)	['θifra]
number	**número** (m)	['numero]
minus sign	**menos** (m)	['menos]
plus sign	**más** (m)	[mas]
sum, total	**suma** (f)	['suma]
first (adj)	**primero** (adj)	[pri'mero]
second (adj)	**segundo** (adj)	[se'ɣundo]
third (adj)	**tercero** (adj)	[ter'θero]
0 zero	**cero**	['θero]
1 one	**uno**	['uno]
2 two	**dos**	[dos]
3 three	**tres**	[tres]
4 four	**cuatro**	[ku'atro]
5 five	**cinco**	['θiŋko]
6 six	**seis**	['sejs]
7 seven	**siete**	['sjete]
8 eight	**ocho**	['otʃo]
9 nine	**nueve**	[nu'eβe]
10 ten	**diez**	[djeθ]
11 eleven	**once**	['onθe]
12 twelve	**doce**	['doθe]
13 thirteen	**trece**	['treθe]
14 fourteen	**catorce**	[ka'torθe]
15 fifteen	**quince**	['kinθe]
16 sixteen	**dieciséis**	['djeθi·s'ejs]
17 seventeen	**diecisiete**	['djeθi·'sjete]

| 18 eighteen | dieciocho | ['djeθi·'otʃo] |
| 19 nineteen | diecinueve | ['djeθi·nu'eβe] |

20 twenty	veinte	['bejnte]
30 thirty	treinta	['trejnta]
40 forty	cuarenta	[kua'renta]
50 fifty	cincuenta	[θiŋku'enta]

60 sixty	sesenta	[se'senta]
70 seventy	setenta	[se'tenta]
80 eighty	ochenta	[o'tʃenta]
90 ninety	noventa	[no'βenta]

100 one hundred	cien	[θjen]
200 two hundred	doscientos	[doθ·'θjentos]
300 three hundred	trescientos	[treθ·'θjentos]
400 four hundred	cuatrocientos	[ku'atro·'θjentos]
500 five hundred	quinientos	[ki'njentos]

600 six hundred	seiscientos	[sejs·'θjentos]
700 seven hundred	setecientos	[θete·'θjentos]
800 eight hundred	ochocientos	[otʃo·'θjentos]
900 nine hundred	novecientos	[noβe·'θjentos]
1000 one thousand	mil	[milʲ]

| 10000 ten thousand | diez mil | ['djeθ 'milʲ] |
| one hundred thousand | cien mil | ['θjen 'milʲ] |

| million | millón (m) | [mi'jon] |
| billion | mil millones | [milʲ mi'jones] |

3. Humans. Family

man (adult male)	hombre (m)	['ombre]
young man	joven (m)	['χoβen]
teenager	adolescente (m)	[aðole'θente]
woman	mujer (f)	[mu'χer]
girl (young woman)	muchacha (f)	[mu'tʃatʃa]

age	edad (f)	[e'ðað]
adult (adj)	adulto	[a'ðulʲto]
middle-aged (adj)	de edad media (adj)	[de e'ðað 'meðja]
elderly (adj)	de edad, anciano (adj)	[de e'ðað], [an'θjano]
old (adj)	viejo (adj)	['bjeχo]

old man	anciano (m)	[an'θjano]
old woman	anciana (f)	[an'θjana]
to retire (from job)	jubilarse (vr)	[χuβi'lʲarse]
retiree	jubilado (m)	[χuβi'lʲaðo]
mother	madre (f)	['maðre]

father	**padre** (m)	['paðre]
son	**hijo** (m)	['iχo]
daughter	**hija** (f)	['iχa]
brother	**hermano** (m)	[er'mano]
sister	**hermana** (f)	[er'mana]
parents	**padres** (m pl)	['paðres]
child	**niño** (m), **niña** (f)	['ninjo], ['ninja]
children	**niños** (m pl)	['ninjos]
stepmother	**madrastra** (f)	[ma'ðrastra]
stepfather	**padrastro** (m)	[pa'ðrastro]
grandmother	**abuela** (f)	[aβu'elʲa]
grandfather	**abuelo** (m)	[aβu'elo]
grandson	**nieto** (m)	['njeto]
granddaughter	**nieta** (f)	['njeta]
grandchildren	**nietos** (m pl)	['njetos]
uncle	**tío** (m)	['tio]
aunt	**tía** (f)	['tia]
nephew	**sobrino** (m)	[so'βrino]
niece	**sobrina** (f)	[so'βrina]
wife	**mujer** (f)	[mu'χer]
husband	**marido** (m)	[ma'riðo]
married (masc.)	**casado** (adj)	[ka'saðo]
married (fem.)	**casada** (adj)	[ka'saða]
widow	**viuda** (f)	['bjuða]
widower	**viudo** (m)	['bjuðo]
name (first name)	**nombre** (m)	['nombre]
surname (last name)	**apellido** (m)	[ape'jiðo]
relative	**pariente** (m)	[pa'rjente]
friend (masc.)	**amigo** (m)	[a'miɣo]
friendship	**amistad** (f)	[amis'tað]
partner	**compañero** (m)	[kompa'njero]
superior (n)	**superior** (m)	[supe'rjor]
colleague	**colega** (m, f)	[ko'leɣa]
neighbors	**vecinos** (m pl)	[be'θinos]

4. Human body

organism (body)	**organismo** (m)	[orɣa'nismo]
body	**cuerpo** (m)	[ku'erpo]
heart	**corazón** (m)	[kora'θon]
blood	**sangre** (f)	['sangre]
brain	**cerebro** (m)	[θe'reβro]
nerve	**nervio** (m)	['nerβjo]

bone	**hueso** (m)	[u'eso]
skeleton	**esqueleto** (m)	[eske'leto]
spine (backbone)	**columna** (f) **vertebral**	[ko'lʲumna berte'βralʲ]
rib	**costilla** (f)	[kos'tija]
skull	**cráneo** (m)	['kraneo]
muscle	**músculo** (m)	['muskulo]
lungs	**pulmones** (m pl)	[pulʲ'mones]
skin	**piel** (f)	[pjelʲ]
head	**cabeza** (f)	[ka'βeθa]
face	**cara** (f)	['kara]
nose	**nariz** (f)	[na'riθ]
forehead	**frente** (f)	['frente]
cheek	**mejilla** (f)	[me'χija]
mouth	**boca** (f)	['boka]
tongue	**lengua** (f)	['lengua]
tooth	**diente** (m)	['djente]
lips	**labios** (m pl)	['lʲaβjos]
chin	**mentón** (m)	[men'ton]
ear	**oreja** (f)	[o'reχa]
neck	**cuello** (m)	[ku'ejo]
throat	**garganta** (f)	[gar'ɣanta]
eye	**ojo** (m)	['oχo]
pupil	**pupila** (f)	[pu'pilʲa]
eyebrow	**ceja** (f)	['θeχa]
eyelash	**pestaña** (f)	[pes'tanja]
hair	**pelo, cabello** (m)	['pelo], [ka'βejo]
hairstyle	**peinado** (m)	[pej'naðo]
mustache	**bigote** (m)	[bi'ɣote]
beard	**barba** (f)	['barβa]
to have (a beard, etc.)	**tener** (vt)	[te'ner]
bald (adj)	**calvo** (adj)	['kalʲβo]
hand	**mano** (f)	['mano]
arm	**brazo** (m)	['braθo]
finger	**dedo** (m)	['deðo]
nail	**uña** (f)	['unja]
palm	**palma** (f)	['palʲma]
shoulder	**hombro** (m)	['ombro]
leg	**pierna** (f)	['pjerna]
foot	**planta** (f)	['plʲanta]
knee	**rodilla** (f)	[ro'ðija]
heel	**talón** (m)	[ta'lon]
back	**espalda** (f)	[es'palʲða]
waist	**cintura** (f), **talle** (m)	[θin'tura], ['taje]

beauty mark	lunar (m)	[luˈnar]
birthmark	marca (f) de nacimiento	[ˈmarka de naθiˈmjento]
(café au lait spot)		

5. Medicine. Diseases. Drugs

health	salud (f)	[saˈluð]
well (not sick)	sano (adj)	[ˈsano]
sickness	enfermedad (f)	[emˌfermeˈðað]
to be sick	estar enfermo	[esˈtar emˌˈfermo]
ill, sick (adj)	enfermo (adj)	[emˌˈfermo]

cold (illness)	resfriado (m)	[resfriˈaðo]
to catch a cold	resfriarse (vr)	[resfriˈarse]
tonsillitis	angina (f)	[anˈxina]
pneumonia	pulmonía (f)	[pulˈmoˈnia]
flu, influenza	gripe (f)	[ˈgripe]

runny nose (coryza)	resfriado (m)	[resfriˈaðo]
cough	tos (f)	[tos]
to cough (vi)	toser (vi)	[toˈser]
to sneeze (vi)	estornudar (vi)	[estornuˈðar]

stroke	insulto (m)	[inˈsulto]
heart attack	ataque (m) cardiaco	[aˈtake karˈðjako]
allergy	alergia (f)	[aˈlerxja]
asthma	asma (f)	[ˈasma]
diabetes	diabetes (m)	[djaˈβetes]

tumor	tumor (m)	[tuˈmor]
cancer	cáncer (m)	[ˈkanθer]
alcoholism	alcoholismo (m)	[alˈkooˈlismo]
AIDS	SIDA (f)	[ˈsiða]
fever	fiebre (f)	[ˈfjeβre]
seasickness	mareo (m)	[maˈreo]

bruise (hématome)	moradura (f)	[moraˈðura]
bump (lump)	chichón (m)	[tʃiˈtʃon]
to limp (vi)	cojear (vi)	[koxeˈar]
dislocation	dislocación (f)	[dislokaˈθjon]
to dislocate (vt)	dislocar (vt)	[disloˈkar]

fracture	fractura (f)	[frakˈtura]
burn (injury)	quemadura (f)	[kemaˈðura]
injury	herida (f)	[eˈriða]
pain, ache	dolor (m)	[doˈlor]
toothache	dolor (m) de muelas	[doˈlor de muˈelas]

| to sweat (perspire) | sudar (vi) | [suˈðar] |
| deaf (adj) | sordo (adj) | [ˈsorðo] |

mute (adj)	mudo (adj)	['muðo]
immunity	inmunidad (f)	[inmuni'ðað]
virus	virus (m)	['birus]
microbe	microbio (m)	[mi'kroβjo]
bacterium	bacteria (f)	[bak'terja]
infection	infección (f)	[iɱfek'θjon]

hospital	hospital (m)	[ospi'talˡ]
cure	cura (f)	['kura]
to vaccinate (vt)	vacunar (vt)	[baku'nar]
to be in a coma	estar en coma	[es'tar en 'koma]
intensive care	revitalización (f)	[reβitaliθa'θjon]
symptom	síntoma (m)	['sintoma]
pulse	pulso (m)	['pulˡso]

6. Feelings. Emotions. Conversation

I, me	yo	[jo]
you	tú	[tu]
he	él	[elˡ]
she	ella	['eja]

we (masc.)	nosotros	[no'sotros]
we (fem.)	nosotras	[no'sotras]
you (masc.)	vosotros	[bo'sotros]
you (fem.)	vosotras	[bo'sotras]
you (polite, sing.)	Usted	[us'teð]
you (polite, pl)	Ustedes	[us'teðes]
they (masc.)	ellos	['ejos]
they (fem.)	ellas	['ejas]

Hello! (fam.)	¡Hola!	['olˡa]
Hello! (form.)	¡Hola!	['olˡa]
Good morning!	¡Buenos días!	['buenos 'dias]
Good afternoon!	¡Buenas tardes!	['buenas 'tarðes]
Good evening!	¡Buenas noches!	['buenas 'notʃes]

to say hello	decir hola	[de'θir 'olˡa]
to greet (vt)	saludar (vt)	[salˡu'ðar]
How are you?	¿Cómo estás?	['komo es'tas]
Goodbye!	¡Adiós!	[a'ðjos]
Bye!	¡Hasta la vista!	['asta lˡa 'bista]
Thank you!	¡Gracias!	['graθjas]

feelings	sentimientos (m pl)	[senti'mjentos]
to be hungry	tener hambre	[te'ner 'ambre]
to be thirsty	tener sed	[te'ner 'seð]
tired (adj)	cansado (adj)	[kan'saðo]
to be worried	inquietarse (vr)	[inkje'tarse]
to be nervous	estar nervioso	[es'tar ner'βjoso]

| hope | esperanza (f) | [espe'ranθa] |
| to hope (vi, vt) | esperar (vi) | [espe'rar] |

character	carácter (m)	[ka'rakter]
modest (adj)	modesto (adj)	[mo'ðesto]
lazy (adj)	perezoso (adj)	[pere'θoso]
generous (adj)	generoso (adj)	[xene'roso]
talented (adj)	talentoso (adj)	[talen'toso]

honest (adj)	honesto (adj)	[o'nesto]
serious (adj)	serio (adj)	['serjo]
shy, timid (adj)	tímido (adj)	['timiðo]
sincere (adj)	sincero (adj)	[sin'θero]
coward	cobarde (m)	[ko'βarðe]

to sleep (vi)	dormir (vi)	[dor'mir]
dream	sueño (m)	[su'enjo]
bed	cama (f)	['kama]
pillow	almohada (f)	[alʲmo'aða]

insomnia	insomnio (m)	[in'somnjo]
to go to bed	irse a la cama	['irse a lʲa 'kama]
nightmare	pesadilla (f)	[pesa'ðija]
alarm clock	despertador (m)	[desperta'ðor]

smile	sonrisa (f)	[son'risa]
to smile (vi)	sonreír (vi)	[sonre'ir]
to laugh (vi)	reírse (vr)	[re'irse]

quarrel	riña (f)	['rinja]
insult	insulto (m)	[in'sulʲto]
resentment	ofensa (f)	[o'fensa]
angry (mad)	enfadado (adj)	[eɱfa'ðaðo]

7. Clothing. Personal accessories

clothes	ropa (f), vestido (m)	['ropa], [bes'tiðo]
coat (overcoat)	abrigo (m)	[a'βriɣo]
fur coat	abrigo (m) de piel	[a'βriɣo de pjelʲ]
jacket (e.g., leather ~)	cazadora (f)	[kaθa'ðora]
raincoat (trenchcoat, etc.)	impermeable (m)	[imperme'aβle]

shirt (button shirt)	camisa (f)	[ka'misa]
pants	pantalones (m pl)	[panta'lones]
suit jacket	chaqueta (f), saco (m)	[tʃa'keta], ['sako]
suit	traje (m)	['traxe]

dress (frock)	vestido (m)	[bes'tiðo]
skirt	falda (f)	['falʲða]
T-shirt	camiseta (f)	[kami'seta]

bathrobe	**bata** (f) **de baño**	['bata de 'baɲo]
pajamas	**pijama** (f)	[pi'xama]
workwear	**ropa** (f) **de trabajo**	['ropa de tra'βaxo]

underwear	**ropa** (f) **interior**	['ropa inte'rjor]
socks	**calcetines** (m pl)	[kalʲθe'tines]
bra	**sostén** (m)	[sos'ten]
pantyhose	**pantimedias** (f pl)	[panti'meðjas]
stockings (thigh highs)	**medias** (f pl)	['meðjas]
bathing suit	**traje** (m) **de baño**	['traxe de 'baɲo]

hat	**gorro** (m)	['goro]
footwear	**calzado** (m)	[kalʲ'θaðo]
boots (e.g., cowboy ~)	**botas** (f pl)	['botas]
heel	**tacón** (m)	[ta'kon]
shoestring	**cordón** (m)	[kor'ðon]
shoe polish	**betún** (m)	[be'tun]

cotton (n)	**algodón** (m)	[alʲɣo'ðon]
wool (n)	**lana** (f)	['lʲana]
fur (n)	**piel** (f)	[pjelʲ]
gloves	**guantes** (m pl)	[gu'antes]
mittens	**manoplas** (f pl)	[ma'noplʲas]
scarf (muffler)	**bufanda** (f)	[bu'fanda]
glasses (eyeglasses)	**gafas** (f pl)	['gafas]
umbrella	**paraguas** (m)	[pa'raɣuas]

tie (necktie)	**corbata** (f)	[kor'βata]
handkerchief	**moquero** (m)	[mo'kero]
comb	**peine** (m)	['pejne]
hairbrush	**cepillo** (m) **de pelo**	[θe'pijo de 'pelo]

buckle	**hebilla** (f)	[e'βija]
belt	**cinturón** (m)	[θintu'ron]
purse	**bolso** (m)	['bolʲso]

collar	**cuello** (m)	[ku'ejo]
pocket	**bolsillo** (m)	[bolʲ'sijo]
sleeve	**manga** (f)	['manga]
fly (on trousers)	**bragueta** (f)	[bra'ɣeta]

zipper (fastener)	**cremallera** (f)	[krema'jera]
button	**botón** (m)	[bo'ton]
to get dirty (vi)	**ensuciarse** (vr)	[ensu'θjarse]
stain (mark, spot)	**mancha** (f)	['mantʃa]

8. City. Urban institutions

| store | **tienda** (f) | ['tjenda] |
| shopping mall | **centro** (m) **comercial** | ['θentro komer'θjalʲ] |

supermarket	**supermercado** (m)	[supermer'kaðo]
shoe store	**zapatería** (f)	[θapate'ria]
bookstore	**librería** (f)	[liβre'ria]

drugstore, pharmacy	**farmacia** (f)	[far'maθja]
bakery	**panadería** (f)	[panaðe'ria]
pastry shop	**pastelería** (f)	[pastele'ria]
grocery store	**tienda** (f) **de comestibles**	['tjenda de komes'tiβles]
butcher shop	**carnicería** (f)	[karni θe'ria]
produce store	**verdulería** (f)	[berðule'ria]
market	**mercado** (m)	[mer'kaðo]

hair salon	**peluquería** (f)	[pelʲuke'ria]
post office	**oficina** (f) **de correos**	[ofi'θina de ko'reos]
dry cleaners	**tintorería** (f)	[tintore'ria]
circus	**circo** (m)	['θirko]
zoo	**zoo** (m)	['θoo]

theater	**teatro** (m)	[te'atro]
movie theater	**cine** (m)	['θine]
museum	**museo** (m)	[mu'seo]
library	**biblioteca** (f)	[biβlio'teka]

mosque	**mezquita** (f)	[meθ'kita]
synagogue	**sinagoga** (f)	[sina'ɣoɣa]
cathedral	**catedral** (f)	[kate'ðralʲ]
temple	**templo** (m)	['templo]
church	**iglesia** (f)	[i'ɣlesja]

college	**instituto** (m)	[insti'tuto]
university	**universidad** (f)	[uniβersi'ðað]
school	**escuela** (f)	[esku'elʲa]

hotel	**hotel** (m)	[o'telʲ]
bank	**banco** (m)	['baŋko]
embassy	**embajada** (f)	[emba'χaða]
travel agency	**agencia** (f) **de viajes**	[a'χenθja de 'bjaχes]

subway	**metro** (m)	['metro]
hospital	**hospital** (m)	[ospi'talʲ]
gas station	**gasolinera** (f)	[gasoli'nera]
parking lot	**aparcamiento** (m)	[aparka'mjento]

ENTRANCE	**ENTRADA**	[en'traða]
EXIT	**SALIDA**	[sa'liða]
PUSH	**EMPUJAR**	[empu'χar]
PULL	**TIRAR**	[ti'rar]
OPEN	**ABIERTO**	[a'βjerto]
CLOSED	**CERRADO**	[θe'raðo]

| monument | **monumento** (m) | [monu'mento] |
| fortress | **fortaleza** (f) | [forta'leθa] |

palace	palacio (m)	[pa'lʲaθjo]
medieval (adj)	medieval (adj)	[meðje'βalʲ]
ancient (adj)	antiguo (adj)	[an'tiɣuo]
national (adj)	nacional (adj)	[naθjo'nalʲ]
famous (monument, etc.)	conocido (adj)	[kono'θiðo]

9. Money. Finances

money	dinero (m)	[di'nero]
coin	moneda (f)	[mo'neða]
dollar	dólar (m)	['dolʲar]
euro	euro (m)	['euro]

ATM	cajero (m) automático	[ka'χero auto'matiko]
currency exchange	oficina (f) de cambio	[ofi'θina de 'kambjo]
exchange rate	curso (m)	['kurso]
cash	dinero (m) en efectivo	[di'nero en efek'tiβo]

How much?	¿cuánto?	[ku'anto]
to pay (vi, vt)	pagar (vi, vt)	[pa'ɣar]
payment	pago (m)	['paɣo]
change (give the ~)	cambio (m)	['kambjo]

price	precio (m)	['preθjo]
discount	descuento (m)	[desku'ento]
cheap (adj)	barato (adj)	[ba'rato]
expensive (adj)	caro (adj)	['karo]

bank	banco (m)	['baŋko]
account	cuenta (f)	[ku'enta]
credit card	tarjeta (f) de crédito	[tar'χeta de 'kreðito]
check	cheque (m)	['tʃeke]
to write a check	sacar un cheque	[sa'kar un 'tʃeke]
checkbook	talonario (m)	[talo'narjo]

debt	deuda (f)	['deuða]
debtor	deudor (m)	[deu'ðor]
to lend (money)	prestar (vt)	[pres'tar]
to borrow (vi, vt)	tomar prestado	[to'mar pres'taðo]

to rent (~ a tuxedo)	alquilar (vt)	[alʲki'lʲar]
on credit (adv)	a crédito (adv)	[a 'kreðito]
wallet	cartera (f)	[kar'tera]
safe	caja (f) fuerte	['kaχa fu'erte]
inheritance	herencia (f)	[e'renθja]
fortune (wealth)	fortuna (f)	[for'tuna]

tax	impuesto (m)	[impu'esto]
fine	multa (f)	['mulʲta]
to fine (vt)	multar (vt)	[mulʲ'tar]

wholesale (adj)	al por mayor (adj)	[alʲ por ma'jor]
retail (adj)	al por menor (adj)	[alʲ por me'nor]
to insure (vt)	asegurar (vt)	[aseɣu'rar]
insurance	seguro (m)	[se'ɣuro]

capital	capital (m)	[kapi'talʲ]
turnover	volumen (m) de negocio	[bo'lʲumen de ne'ɣoθjo]
stock (share)	acción (f)	[ak'θjon]
profit	beneficio (m)	[bene'fiθjo]
profitable (adj)	beneficioso (adj)	[benefi'θjoso]

crisis	crisis (m)	['krisis]
bankruptcy	bancarrota (f)	[baŋka'rota]
to go bankrupt	ir a la bancarrota	[ir a lʲa baŋka'rota]

accountant	contable (m)	[kon'taβle]
salary	salario (m)	[sa'lʲarjo]
bonus (money)	premio (m)	['premjo]

10. Transportation

bus	autobús (m)	[auto'βus]
streetcar	tranvía (m)	[tram'bia]
trolley bus	trolebús (m)	[trole'βus]

to go by ...	ir en ...	[ir en]
to get on (~ the bus)	tomar (vt)	[to'mar]
to get off ...	bajar del ...	[ba'xar delʲ]

stop (e.g., bus ~)	parada (f)	[pa'raða]
terminus	parada (f) final	[pa'raða fi'nalʲ]
schedule	horario (m)	[o'rarjo]
ticket	billete (m)	[bi'jete]
to be late (for ...)	llegar tarde (vi)	[je'ɣar 'tarðe]

taxi, cab	taxi (m)	['taksi]
by taxi	en taxi	[en 'taksi]
taxi stand	parada (f) de taxi	[pa'raða de 'taksi]

traffic	tráfico (m)	['trafiko]
rush hour	horas (f pl) de punta	['oras de 'punta]
to park (vi)	aparcar (vi)	[apar'kar]

subway	metro (m)	['metro]
station	estación (f)	[esta'θjon]
train	tren (m)	['tren]
train station	estación (f)	[esta'θjon]
rails	rieles (m pl)	['rjeles]
compartment	compartimiento (m)	[komparti'mjento]
berth	litera (f)	[li'tera]

airplane	avión (m)	[a'βjon]
air ticket	billete (m) de avión	[bi'jete de a'βjon]
airline	compañía (f) aérea	[kompa'njia a'erea]
airport	aeropuerto (m)	[aeropu'erto]

flight (act of flying)	vuelo (m)	[bu'elo]
luggage	equipaje (m)	[eki'paxe]
luggage cart	carrito (m) de equipaje	[ka'rito de eki'paxe]

ship	buque (m)	['buke]
cruise ship	trasatlántico (m)	[trasat'lʲantiko]
yacht	yate (m)	['jate]
boat (flat-bottomed ~)	bote (m)	['bote]

captain	capitán (m)	[kapi'tan]
cabin	camarote (m)	[kama'rote]
port (harbor)	puerto (m)	[pu'erto]

bicycle	bicicleta (f)	[biθik'leta]
scooter	scooter (f)	[es'kuter]
motorcycle, bike	motocicleta (f)	[motoθi'kleta]
pedal	pedal (m)	[pe'ðalʲ]
pump	bomba (f)	['bomba]
wheel	rueda (f)	[ru'eða]

automobile, car	coche (m)	['kotʃe]
ambulance	ambulancia (f)	[ambu'lʲanθja]
truck	camión (m)	[ka'mjon]
used (adj)	de ocasión (adj)	[de oka'θjon]
car crash	accidente (m)	[akθi'ðente]
repair	reparación (f)	[repara'θjon]

11. Food. Part 1

meat	carne (f)	['karne]
chicken	gallina (f)	[ga'jina]
duck	pato (m)	['pato]

pork	carne (f) de cerdo	['karne de 'θerðo]
veal	carne (f) de ternera	['karne de ter'nera]
lamb	carne (f) de carnero	['karne de kar'nero]
beef	carne (f) de vaca	['karne de 'baka]

| sausage (bologna, pepperoni, etc.) | salchichón (m) | [salʲtʃi'tʃon] |

egg	huevo (m)	[u'eβo]
fish	pescado (m)	[pes'kaðo]
cheese	queso (m)	['keso]
sugar	azúcar (m)	[a'θukar]
salt	sal (f)	[salʲ]

rice	arroz (m)	[a'roθ]
pasta (macaroni)	macarrones (m pl)	[maka'rones]
butter	mantequilla (f)	[mante'kija]
vegetable oil	aceite (m) vegetal	[a'θejte beχe'talʲ]
bread	pan (m)	[pan]
chocolate (n)	chocolate (m)	[tʃoko'lʲate]
wine	vino (m)	['bino]
coffee	café (m)	[ka'fe]
milk	leche (f)	['letʃe]
juice	zumo (m), jugo (m)	['θumo], ['χuɣo]
beer	cerveza (f)	[θer'βeθa]
tea	té (m)	[te]
tomato	tomate (m)	[to'mate]
cucumber	pepino (m)	[pe'pino]
carrot	zanahoria (f)	[θana'orja]
potato	patata (f)	[pa'tata]
onion	cebolla (f)	[θe'βoja]
garlic	ajo (m)	['aχo]
cabbage	col (f)	[kolʲ]
beetroot	remolacha (f)	[remo'lʲatʃa]
eggplant	berenjena (f)	[beren'χena]
dill	eneldo (m)	[e'nelʲðo]
lettuce	lechuga (f)	[le'tʃuɣa]
corn (maize)	maíz (m)	[ma'iθ]
fruit	fruto (m)	['fruto]
apple	manzana (f)	[man'θana]
pear	pera (f)	['pera]
lemon	limón (m)	[li'mon]
orange	naranja (f)	[na'ranχa]
strawberry (garden ~)	fresa (f)	['fresa]
plum	ciruela (f)	[θiru'elʲa]
raspberry	frambuesa (f)	[frambu'esa]
pineapple	ananás (m)	[ana'nas]
banana	banana (f)	[ba'nana]
watermelon	sandía (f)	[san'dia]
grape	uva (f)	['uβa]
melon	melón (m)	[me'lon]

12. Food. Part 2

cuisine	cocina (f)	[ko'θina]
recipe	receta (f)	[re'θeta]
food	comida (f)	[ko'miða]
to have breakfast	desayunar (vi)	[desaju'nar]
to have lunch	almorzar (vi)	[alʲmor'θar]

to have dinner	**cenar** (vi)	[θe'nar]
taste, flavor	**sabor** (m)	[sa'βor]
tasty (adj)	**sabroso** (adj)	[sa'βroso]
cold (adj)	**frío** (adj)	['frio]
hot (adj)	**caliente** (adj)	[ka'ljente]
sweet (sugary)	**azucarado, dulce** (adj)	[aθuka'raðo], ['dulʲθe]
salty (adj)	**salado** (adj)	[sa'lʲaðo]
sandwich (bread)	**bocadillo** (m)	[boka'ðijo]
side dish	**guarnición** (f)	[guarni'θjon]
filling (for cake, pie)	**relleno** (m)	[re'jeno]
sauce	**salsa** (f)	['salʲsa]
piece (of cake, pie)	**pedazo** (m)	[pe'ðaθo]
diet	**dieta** (f)	[di'eta]
vitamin	**vitamina** (f)	[bita'mina]
calorie	**caloría** (f)	[kalo'ria]
vegetarian (n)	**vegetariano** (m)	[beχeta'rjano]
restaurant	**restaurante** (m)	[restau'rante]
coffee house	**cafetería** (f)	[kafete'ria]
appetite	**apetito** (m)	[ape'tito]
Enjoy your meal!	**¡Que aproveche!**	[ke apro'βetʃe]
waiter	**camarero** (m)	[kama'rero]
waitress	**camarera** (f)	[kama'rera]
bartender	**barman** (m)	['barman]
menu	**carta** (f), **menú** (m)	['karta], [me'nu]
spoon	**cuchara** (f)	[ku'tʃara]
knife	**cuchillo** (m)	[ku'tʃijo]
fork	**tenedor** (m)	[tene'ðor]
cup (e.g., coffee ~)	**taza** (f)	['taθa]
plate (dinner ~)	**plato** (m)	['plʲato]
saucer	**platillo** (m)	[plʲa'tijo]
napkin (on table)	**servilleta** (f)	[serβi'jeta]
toothpick	**mondadientes** (m)	[monda'ðjentes]
to order (meal)	**pedir** (vt)	[pe'ðir]
course, dish	**plato** (m)	['plʲato]
portion	**porción** (f)	[por'θjon]
appetizer	**entremés** (m)	[entre'mes]
salad	**ensalada** (f)	[ensa'lʲaða]
soup	**sopa** (f)	['sopa]
dessert	**postre** (m)	['postre]
jam (whole fruit jam)	**confitura** (f)	[komfi'tura]
ice-cream	**helado** (m)	[e'lʲaðo]
check	**cuenta** (f)	[ku'enta]
to pay the check	**pagar la cuenta**	[pa'ɣar lʲa ku'enta]
tip	**propina** (f)	[pro'pina]

13. House. Apartment. Part 1

house	casa (f)	['kasa]
country house	casa (f) de campo	['kasa de 'kampo]
villa (seaside ~)	villa (f)	['bija]
floor, story	piso (m)	['piso]
entrance	entrada (f)	[en'traða]
wall	pared (f)	[pa'reð]
roof	techo (m)	['tetʃo]
chimney	chimenea (f)	[tʃime'nea]
attic (storage place)	desván (m)	[des'βan]
window	ventana (f)	[ben'tana]
window ledge	alféizar (m)	[al'fejθar]
balcony	balcón (m)	[balʲ'kon]
stairs (stairway)	escalera (f)	[eska'lera]
mailbox	buzón (m)	[bu'θon]
garbage can	contenedor (m) de basura	[kontene'ðor de ba'sura]
elevator	ascensor (m)	[aθen'sor]
electricity	electricidad (f)	[elektriθi'ðað]
light bulb	bombilla (f)	[bom'bija]
switch	interruptor (m)	[interup'tor]
wall socket	enchufe (m)	[en'tʃufe]
fuse	fusible (m)	[fu'siβle]
door	puerta (f)	[pu'erta]
handle, doorknob	tirador (m)	[tira'ðor]
key	llave (f)	['jaβe]
doormat	felpudo (m)	[felʲ'puðo]
door lock	cerradura (f)	[θera'ðura]
doorbell	timbre (m)	['timbre]
knock (at the door)	llamada (f)	[ja'maða]
to knock (vi)	llamar (vi)	[ja'mar]
peephole	mirilla (f)	[mi'rija]
yard	patio (m)	['patjo]
garden	jardín (m)	[χar'ðin]
swimming pool	piscina (f)	[pi'θina]
gym (home gym)	gimnasio (m)	[χim'nasjo]
tennis court	cancha (f) de tenis	['kantʃa de 'tenis]
garage	garaje (m)	[ga'raχe]
private property	propiedad (f) privada	[propje'ðað pri'βaða]
warning sign	letrero (m) de aviso	[le'trero de a'βiθo]
security	seguridad (f)	[seɣuri'ðað]
security guard	guardia (m) de seguridad	[gu'arðja de seɣuri'ðað]
renovations	renovación (f)	[renoβa'θjon]

to renovate (vt)	renovar (vt)	[reno'βar]
to put in order	poner en orden	[po'ner en 'orðen]
to paint (~ a wall)	pintar (vt)	[pin'tar]
wallpaper	empapelado (m)	[empape'l'aðo]
to varnish (vt)	cubrir con barniz	[ku'βrir kon bar'niθ]

pipe	tubo (m)	['tuβo]
tools	instrumentos (m pl)	[instru'mentos]
basement	sótano (m)	['sotano]
sewerage (system)	alcantarillado (m)	[al'kantari'jaðo]

14. House. Apartment. Part 2

apartment	apartamento (m)	[aparta'mento]
room	habitación (f)	[aβita'θjon]
bedroom	dormitorio (m)	[dormi'torjo]
dining room	comedor (m)	[kome'ðor]

living room	salón (m)	[sa'lon]
study (home office)	despacho (m)	[des'patʃo]
entry room	antecámara (f)	[ante'kamara]
bathroom (room with a bath or shower)	cuarto (m) de baño	[ku'arto de 'banjo]
half bath	servicio (m)	[ser'βiθjo]

floor	suelo (m)	[su'elo]
ceiling	techo (m)	['tetʃo]
to dust (vt)	limpiar el polvo	[lim'pjar el' 'pol'βo]
vacuum cleaner	aspirador (m)	[aspira'ðor]
to vacuum (vt)	limpiar con la aspiradora	[lim'pjar kon l'a aspira'ðora]

mop	fregona (f)	[fre'ɣona]
dust cloth	trapo (m)	['trapo]
short broom	escoba (f)	[es'koβa]
dustpan	cogedor (m)	[koχe'ðor]

furniture	muebles (m pl)	[mu'eβles]
table	mesa (f)	['mesa]
chair	silla (f)	['sija]
armchair	sillón (m)	[si'jon]

bookcase	librería (f)	[liβre'ria]
shelf	estante (m)	[es'tante]
wardrobe	armario (m)	[ar'marjo]

mirror	espejo (m)	[es'peχo]
carpet	tapiz (m)	[ta'piθ]
fireplace	chimenea (f)	[tʃime'nea]
drapes	cortinas (f pl)	[kor'tinas]

table lamp	lámpara (f) de mesa	['lampara de 'mesa]
chandelier	lámpara (f) de araña	['lampara de a'ranja]

kitchen	cocina (f)	[ko'θina]
gas stove (range)	cocina (f) de gas	[ko'θina de 'gas]
electric stove	cocina (f) eléctrica	[ko'θina e'lektrika]
microwave oven	horno (m) microondas	['orno mikro·'ondas]

refrigerator	frigorífico (m)	[friɣo'rifiko]
freezer	congelador (m)	[konχela'ðor]
dishwasher	lavavajillas (m)	['laβa·βa'χijas]
faucet	grifo (m)	['grifo]

meat grinder	picadora (f) de carne	[pika'ðora de 'karne]
juicer	exprimidor (m)	[eksprimi'ðor]
toaster	tostador (m)	[tosta'ðor]
mixer	batidora (f)	[bati'ðora]

coffee machine	cafetera (f)	[kafe'tera]
kettle	hervidor (m) de agua	[erβi'ðor de 'aɣua]
teapot	tetera (f)	[te'tera]

TV set	televisor (m)	[teleβi'sor]
VCR (video recorder)	vídeo (m)	['biðeo]
iron (e.g., steam ~)	plancha (f)	['plantʃa]
telephone	teléfono (m)	[te'lefono]

15. Professions. Social status

director	director (m)	[direk'tor]
superior	superior (m)	[supe'rjor]
president	presidente (m)	[presi'ðente]
assistant	asistente (m)	[asis'tente]
secretary	secretario (m), secretaria (f)	[sekre'tarjo], [sekre'tarja]

owner, proprietor	propietario (m)	[propje'tarjo]
partner	compañero (m)	[kompa'njero]
stockholder	accionista (m)	[akθjo'nista]

businessman	hombre (m) de negocios	['ombre de ne'ɣoθjos]
millionaire	millonario (m)	[mijo'narjo]
billionaire	multimillonario (m)	[multi·mijo'narjo]

actor	actor (m)	[ak'tor]
architect	arquitecto (m)	[arki'tekto]
banker	banquero (m)	[baŋ'kero]
broker	broker (m)	['broker]
veterinarian	veterinario (m)	[beteri'narjo]
doctor	médico (m)	['meðiko]

chambermaid	camarera (f)	[kama'rera]
designer	diseñador (m)	[disenja'ðor]
correspondent	corresponsal (m)	[korespon'salʲ]
delivery man	repartidor (m)	[reparti'ðor]
electrician	electricista (m)	[elektri'θista]
musician	músico (m)	['musiko]
babysitter	niñera (f)	[ni'njera]
hairdresser	peluquero (m)	[pelʲu'kero]
herder, shepherd	pastor (m)	[pas'tor]
singer (masc.)	cantante (m)	[kan'tante]
translator	traductor (m)	[traðuk'tor]
writer	escritor (m)	[eskri'tor]
carpenter	carpintero (m)	[karpin'tero]
cook	cocinero (m)	[koθi'nero]
fireman	bombero (m)	[bom'bero]
police officer	policía (m)	[poli'θia]
mailman	cartero (m)	[kar'tero]
programmer	programador (m)	[proɣrama'ðor]
salesman (store staff)	vendedor (m)	[bende'ðor]
worker	obrero (m)	[o'βrero]
gardener	jardinero (m)	[χarði'nero]
plumber	fontanero (m)	[fonta'nero]
dentist	estomatólogo (m)	[estoma'toloɣo]
flight attendant (fem.)	azafata (f)	[aθa'fata]
dancer (masc.)	bailarín (m)	[bajlʲa'rin]
bodyguard	guardaespaldas (m)	[guarða·es'palʲðas]
scientist	científico (m)	[θjen'tifiko]
schoolteacher	profesor (m)	[profe'sor]
farmer	granjero (m)	[gran'χero]
surgeon	cirujano (m)	[θiru'χano]
miner	minero (m)	[mi'nero]
chef (kitchen chef)	jefe (m) de cocina	['χefe de ko'θina]
driver	chófer (m)	['tʃofer]

16. Sport

kind of sports	tipo (m) de deporte	['tipo de de'porte]
soccer	fútbol (m)	['futβolʲ]
hockey	hockey (m)	['χokej]
basketball	baloncesto (m)	[balon'θesto]
baseball	béisbol (m)	['bejsβol]
volleyball	voleibol (m)	[bolej'βolʲ]
boxing	boxeo (m)	[bo'kseo]

wrestling	**lucha** (f)	['lʲutʃa]
tennis	**tenis** (m)	['tenis]
swimming	**natación** (f)	[nata'θjon]

chess	**ajedrez** (m)	[aχe'ðreθ]
running	**carrera** (f)	[ka'rera]
athletics	**atletismo** (m)	[atle'tismo]
figure skating	**patinaje** (m) **artístico**	[pati'naχe ar'tistiko]
cycling	**ciclismo** (m)	[θik'lismo]

billiards	**billar** (m)	[bi'jar]
bodybuilding	**culturismo** (m)	[kulʲtu'rismo]
golf	**golf** (m)	[golʲf]
scuba diving	**buceo** (m)	[bu'θeo]
sailing	**vela** (f)	['belʲa]
archery	**tiro** (m) **con arco**	['tiro kon 'arko]

period, half	**tiempo** (m)	['tjempo]
half-time	**descanso** (m)	[des'kanso]
tie	**empate** (m)	[em'pate]
to tie (vi)	**empatar** (vi)	[empa'tar]

treadmill	**cinta** (f) **de correr**	['θinta de ko'rer]
player	**jugador** (m)	[χuɣa'ðor]
substitute	**reserva** (m)	[re'serβa]
substitutes bench	**banquillo** (m) **de reserva**	[baŋ'kijo de re'serβa]

match	**match** (m)	[matʃ]
goal	**puerta** (f)	[pu'erta]
goalkeeper	**portero** (m)	[por'tero]
goal (score)	**gol** (m)	[golʲ]

Olympic Games	**Juegos** (m pl) **Olímpicos**	[χu'eɣos o'limpikos]
to set a record	**establecer un record**	[estaβle'θer un 'rekorð]
final	**final** (m)	[fi'nalʲ]
champion	**campeón** (m)	[kampe'on]
championship	**campeonato** (m)	[kampeo'nato]

winner	**vencedor** (m)	[benθe'ðor]
victory	**victoria** (f)	[bik'torja]
to win (vi)	**ganar** (vi)	[ga'njar]
to lose (not win)	**perder** (vi)	[per'ðer]
medal	**medalla** (f)	[me'ðaja]

first place	**primer puesto** (m)	[pri'mer pu'esto]
second place	**segundo puesto** (m)	[se'ɣundo pu'esto]
third place	**tercer puesto** (m)	[ter'θer pu'esto]

stadium	**estadio** (m)	[es'taðjo]
fan, supporter	**hincha** (m)	['intʃa]
trainer, coach	**entrenador** (m)	[entrena'ðor]
training	**entrenamiento** (m)	[entrena'mjento]

17. Foreign languages. Orthography

language	lengua (f)	['lengua]
to study (vt)	estudiar (vt)	[estu'ðjar]
pronunciation	pronunciación (f)	[pronunθja'θjon]
accent	acento (m)	[a'θento]
noun	sustantivo (m)	[sustan'tiβo]
adjective	adjetivo (m)	[aðχe'tiβo]
verb	verbo (m)	['berβo]
adverb	adverbio (m)	[að'βerβjo]
pronoun	pronombre (m)	[pro'nombre]
interjection	interjección (f)	[interχek'θjon]
preposition	preposición (f)	[preposi'θjon]
root	raíz (f), radical (m)	[ra'iθ], [raði'kal]
ending	desinencia (f)	[desi'nenθja]
prefix	prefijo (m)	[pre'fiχo]
syllable	sílaba (f)	['silʲaβa]
suffix	sufijo (m)	[su'fiχo]
stress mark	acento (m)	[a'θento]
period, dot	punto (m)	['punto]
comma	coma (f)	['koma]
colon	dos puntos (m pl)	[dos 'puntos]
ellipsis	puntos (m pl) suspensivos	['puntos suspen'siβos]
question	pregunta (f)	[pre'ɣunta]
question mark	signo (m) de interrogación	['siɣno de interoɣa'θjon]
exclamation point	signo (m) de admiración	['siɣno de aðmira'θjon]
in quotation marks	entre comillas	['entre ko'mijas]
in parenthesis	entre paréntesis	['entre pa'rentesis]
letter	letra (f)	['letra]
capital letter	letra (f) mayúscula	['letra ma'juskulʲa]
sentence	oración (f)	[ora'θjon]
group of words	combinación (f) de palabras	[kombina'θjon de pa'lʲaβras]
expression	expresión (f)	[ekspre'θjon]
subject	sujeto (m)	[su'χeto]
predicate	predicado (m)	[preði'kaðo]
line	línea (f)	['linea]
paragraph	párrafo (m)	['parafo]
synonym	sinónimo (m)	[si'nonimo]
antonym	antónimo (m)	[an'tonimo]

exception	**excepción** (f)	[ekθep'θjon]
to underline (vt)	**subrayar** (vt)	[suβra'jar]
rules	**reglas** (f pl)	['reɣlʲas]
grammar	**gramática** (f)	[gra'matika]
vocabulary	**vocabulario** (m)	[bokaβu'larjo]
phonetics	**fonética** (f)	[fo'netika]
alphabet	**alfabeto** (m)	[alʲfa'βeto]
textbook	**manual** (m)	[manu'alʲ]
dictionary	**diccionario** (m)	[dikθjo'narjo]
phrasebook	**guía** (f) **de conversación**	['gia de kombersa'θjon]
word	**palabra** (f)	[pa'lʲaβra]
meaning	**significado** (m)	[siɣnifi'kaðo]
memory	**memoria** (f)	[me'morja]

18. The Earth. Geography

the Earth	**Tierra** (f)	['tjera]
the globe (the Earth)	**globo** (m) **terrestre**	['gloβo te'restre]
planet	**planeta** (m)	[plʲa'neta]
geography	**geografía** (f)	[xeoɣra'fia]
nature	**naturaleza** (f)	[natura'leθa]
map	**mapa** (m)	['mapa]
atlas	**atlas** (m)	['atlʲas]
in the north	**en el norte**	[en elʲ 'norte]
in the south	**en el sur**	[en elʲ sur]
in the west	**en el oeste**	[en elʲ o'este]
in the east	**en el este**	[en elʲ 'este]
sea	**mar** (m)	[mar]
ocean	**océano** (m)	[o'θeano]
gulf (bay)	**golfo** (m)	['golʲfo]
straits	**estrecho** (m)	[es'tretʃo]
continent (mainland)	**continente** (m)	[konti'nente]
island	**isla** (f)	['islʲa]
peninsula	**península** (f)	[pe'ninsulʲa]
archipelago	**archipiélago** (m)	[artʃipi'elʲaɣo]
harbor	**puerto** (m)	[pu'erto]
coral reef	**arrecife** (m) **de coral**	[are'θife de ko'ralʲ]
shore	**orilla** (f)	[o'rija]
coast	**costa** (f)	['kosta]
flow (flood tide)	**flujo** (m)	['flʲuχo]
ebb (ebb tide)	**reflujo** (m)	[re'flʲuχo]

latitude	latitud (f)	[lʲati'tuð]
longitude	longitud (f)	[lonχi'tuð]
parallel	paralelo (m)	[para'lelo]
equator	ecuador (m)	[ekua'ðor]

sky	cielo (m)	['θjelo]
horizon	horizonte (m)	[ori'θonte]
atmosphere	atmósfera (f)	[að'mosfera]

mountain	montaña (f)	[mon'tanja]
summit, top	cima (f)	['θima]
cliff	roca (f)	['roka]
hill	colina (f)	[ko'lina]

volcano	volcán (m)	[bolʲ'kan]
glacier	glaciar (m)	[glʲa'θjar]
waterfall	cascada (f)	[kas'kaða]
plain	llanura (f)	[ja'nura]

river	río (m)	['rio]
spring (natural source)	manantial (m)	[manan'tjalʲ]
bank (of river)	orilla (f), ribera (f)	[o'rija], [ri'βera]
downstream (adv)	río abajo (adv)	['rio a'βaχo]
upstream (adv)	río arriba (adv)	['rio a'riβa]

lake	lago (m)	['lʲaγo]
dam	presa (f)	['presa]
canal	canal (m)	[ka'nalʲ]
swamp (marshland)	pantano (m)	[pan'tano]
ice	hielo (m)	['jelo]

19. Countries of the world. Part 1

Europe	Europa (f)	[eu'ropa]
European Union	Unión (f) Europea	[u'njon euro'pea]
European (n)	europeo (m)	[euro'peo]
European (adj)	europeo (adj)	[euro'peo]

Austria	Austria (f)	['austrja]
Great Britain	Gran Bretaña (f)	[gran bre'tanja]
England	Inglaterra (f)	[inglʲa'tera]
Belgium	Bélgica (f)	['belʲχika]
Germany	Alemania (f)	[ale'manja]

Netherlands	Países Bajos (m pl)	[pa'ises 'baχos]
Holland	Holanda (f)	[o'lʲanda]
Greece	Grecia (f)	['greθja]
Denmark	Dinamarca (f)	[dina'marka]
Ireland	Irlanda (f)	[ir'lʲanda]
Iceland	Islandia (f)	[is'lʲandja]

Spain	España (f)	[es'paɲa]
Italy	Italia (f)	[i'talja]
Cyprus	Chipre (m)	['tʃipre]
Malta	Malta (f)	['malʲta]

Norway	Noruega (f)	[noru'eɣa]
Portugal	Portugal (f)	[portu'ɣalʲ]
Finland	Finlandia (f)	[fin'lʲandja]
France	Francia (f)	['franθja]
Sweden	Suecia (f)	[su'eθja]

Switzerland	Suiza (f)	[su'isa]
Scotland	Escocia (f)	[es'koθja]
Vatican	Vaticano (m)	[bati'kano]
Liechtenstein	Liechtenstein (m)	[leχten'stejn]
Luxembourg	Luxemburgo (m)	[lʲuksem'burɣo]

Monaco	Mónaco (m)	['monako]
Albania	Albania (f)	[alʲ'βanja]
Bulgaria	Bulgaria (f)	[bul'ɣarja]
Hungary	Hungría (f)	[un'gria]
Latvia	Letonia (f)	[le'tonja]

Lithuania	Lituania (f)	[litu'anja]
Poland	Polonia (f)	[po'lonja]
Romania	Rumania (f)	[ru'manja]
Serbia	Serbia (f)	['serβja]
Slovakia	Eslovaquia (f)	[eslo'βakja]

Croatia	Croacia (f)	[kro'aθja]
Czech Republic	Chequia (f)	['tʃekja]
Estonia	Estonia (f)	[es'tonja]
Bosnia and Herzegovina	Bosnia y Herzegovina	['bosnia i erθeχo'βina]
Macedonia (Republic of ~)	Macedonia	[maθe'ðonja]

Slovenia	Eslovenia	[eslo'βenja]
Montenegro	Montenegro (m)	[monte'neɣro]
Belarus	Bielorrusia (f)	[bjelo'rusja]
Moldova, Moldavia	Moldavia (f)	[molʲ'ðaβja]
Russia	Rusia (f)	['rusja]
Ukraine	Ucrania (f)	[u'kranja]

20. Countries of the world. Part 2

Asia	Asia (f)	['asja]
Vietnam	Vietnam (m)	[bjet'nam]
India	India (f)	['indja]
Israel	Israel (m)	[isra'elʲ]
China	China (f)	['tʃina]
Lebanon	Líbano (m)	['liβano]

Mongolia	**Mongolia** (f)	[mon'golja]
Malaysia	**Malasia** (f)	[ma'lʲasja]
Pakistan	**Pakistán** (m)	[pakis'tan]
Saudi Arabia	**Arabia** (f) **Saudita**	[a'raβja sau'ðita]
Thailand	**Tailandia** (f)	[taj'lʲandja]
Taiwan	**Taiwán** (m)	[taj'wan]
Turkey	**Turquía** (f)	[tur'kia]
Japan	**Japón** (m)	[χa'pon]
Afghanistan	**Afganistán** (m)	[afɣanis'tan]
Bangladesh	**Bangladesh** (m)	[banglʲa'ðeʃ]
Indonesia	**Indonesia** (f)	[indo'nesja]
Jordan	**Jordania** (f)	[χor'ðanja]
Iraq	**Irak** (m)	[i'rak]
Iran	**Irán** (m)	[i'ran]
Cambodia	**Camboya** (f)	[kam'boja]
Kuwait	**Kuwait** (m)	[ku'wajt]
Laos	**Laos** (m)	[lʲa'os]
Myanmar	**Myanmar** (m)	[mjan'mar]
Nepal	**Nepal** (m)	[ne'palʲ]
United Arab Emirates	**Emiratos** (m pl) **Árabes Unidos**	[emi'rates 'araβes u'niðos]
Syria	**Siria** (f)	['sirja]
Palestine	**Palestina** (f)	[pales'tina]
South Korea	**Corea** (f) **del Sur**	[ko'rea delʲ sur]
North Korea	**Corea** (f) **del Norte**	[ko'rea delʲ 'norte]
United States of America	**Estados Unidos de América** (m pl)	[es'tados u'niðos de a'merika]
Canada	**Canadá** (f)	[kana'ða]
Mexico	**Méjico** (m)	['meχiko]
Argentina	**Argentina** (f)	[arχen'tina]
Brazil	**Brasil** (f)	[bra'silʲ]
Colombia	**Colombia** (f)	[ko'lombja]
Cuba	**Cuba** (f)	['kuβa]
Chile	**Chile** (m)	['ʧile]
Venezuela	**Venezuela** (f)	[beneθu'elʲa]
Ecuador	**Ecuador** (m)	[ekua'ðor]
The Bahamas	**Islas** (f pl) **Bahamas**	['islʲas ba'amas]
Panama	**Panamá** (f)	[pana'ma]
Egypt	**Egipto** (m)	[e'χipto]
Morocco	**Marruecos** (m)	[maru'ekos]
Tunisia	**Túnez** (m)	['tuneθ]
Kenya	**Kenia** (f)	['kenja]
Libya	**Libia** (f)	['liβja]
South Africa	**República** (f) **Sudafricana**	[re'puβlika suð·afri'kana]

| Australia | **Australia** (f) | [aus'tralja] |
| New Zealand | **Nueva Zelanda** (f) | [nu'eβa θe'lʲanda] |

21. Weather. Natural disasters

weather	**tiempo** (m)	['tjempo]
weather forecast	**previsión** (m) **del tiempo**	[preβi'sjon delʲ 'tjempo]
temperature	**temperatura** (f)	[tempera'tura]
thermometer	**termómetro** (m)	[ter'mometro]
barometer	**barómetro** (m)	[ba'rometro]
sun	**sol** (m)	[solʲ]
to shine (vi)	**brillar** (vi)	[bri'jar]
sunny (day)	**soleado** (adj)	[sole'aðo]
to come up (vi)	**elevarse** (vr)	[ele'βarse]
to set (vi)	**ponerse** (vr)	[po'nerse]
rain	**lluvia** (f)	['juβja]
it's raining	**está lloviendo**	[es'ta jo'βjendo]
pouring rain	**aguacero** (m)	[aɣua'θero]
rain cloud	**nubarrón** (m)	[nuβa'ron]
puddle	**charco** (m)	['tʃarko]
to get wet (in rain)	**mojarse** (vr)	[mo'xarse]
thunderstorm	**tormenta** (f)	[tor'menta]
lightning (~ strike)	**relámpago** (m)	[re'lʲampaɣo]
to flash (vi)	**relampaguear** (vi)	[relʲampaɣe'ar]
thunder	**trueno** (m)	[tru'eno]
it's thundering	**está tronando**	[es'ta tro'nando]
hail	**granizo** (m)	[gra'niθo]
it's hailing	**está granizando**	[es'ta grani'θando]
heat (extreme ~)	**bochorno** (m)	[bo'tʃorno]
it's hot	**hace mucho calor**	['aθe 'mutʃo ka'lor]
it's warm	**hace calor**	['aθe ka'lor]
it's cold	**hace frío**	['aθe 'frio]
fog (mist)	**niebla** (f)	['njeβlʲa]
foggy	**nebuloso** (adj)	[neβu'loso]
cloud	**nube** (f)	['nuβe]
cloudy (adj)	**nuboso** (adj)	[nu'βoso]
humidity	**humedad** (f)	[ume'ðað]
snow	**nieve** (f)	['njeβe]
it's snowing	**está nevando**	[es'ta ne'βando]
frost (severe ~, freezing cold)	**helada** (f)	[e'lʲaða]
below zero (adv)	**bajo cero** (adv)	['baxo 'θero]
hoarfrost	**escarcha** (f)	[es'kartʃa]
bad weather	**mal tiempo** (m)	[malʲ 'tjempo]

disaster	catástrofe (f)	[ka'tastrofe]
flood, inundation	inundación (f)	[inunda'θjon]
avalanche	avalancha (f)	[aβa'ʎantʃa]
earthquake	terremoto (m)	[tere'moto]

tremor, quake	sacudida (f)	[saku'ðiða]
epicenter	epicentro (m)	[epi'θentro]
eruption	erupción (f)	[erup'θjon]
lava	lava (f)	['ʎaβa]

tornado	tornado (m)	[tor'naðo]
twister	torbellino (m)	[torβe'jino]
hurricane	huracán (m)	[ura'kan]
tsunami	tsunami (m)	[tsu'nami]
cyclone	ciclón (m)	[θik'lon]

22. Animals. Part 1

| animal | animal (m) | [ani'maʎ] |
| predator | carnívoro (m) | [kar'niβoro] |

tiger	tigre (m)	['tiɣre]
lion	león (m)	[le'on]
wolf	lobo (m)	['loβo]
fox	zorro (m)	['θoro]
jaguar	jaguar (m)	[xaɣu'ar]

lynx	lince (m)	['linθe]
coyote	coyote (m)	[ko'jote]
jackal	chacal (m)	[tʃa'kaʎ]
hyena	hiena (f)	['jena]

squirrel	ardilla (f)	[ar'ðija]
hedgehog	erizo (m)	[e'riθo]
rabbit	conejo (m)	[ko'nexo]
raccoon	mapache (m)	[ma'patʃe]

hamster	hámster (m)	['amster]
mole	topo (m)	['topo]
mouse	ratón (m)	[ra'ton]
rat	rata (f)	['rata]
bat	murciélago (m)	[mur'θjelaɣo]

beaver	castor (m)	[kas'tor]
horse	caballo (m)	[ka'βajo]
deer	ciervo (m)	['θjerβo]
camel	camello (m)	[ka'mejo]
zebra	cebra (f)	['θeβra]
whale	ballena (f)	[ba'jena]
seal	foca (f)	['foka]

| walrus | morsa (f) | ['morsa] |
| dolphin | delfín (m) | [delⁱ'fin] |

bear	oso (m)	['oso]
monkey	mono (m)	['mono]
elephant	elefante (m)	[ele'fante]
rhinoceros	rinoceronte (m)	[rinoθe'ronte]
giraffe	jirafa (f)	[χi'rafa]

hippopotamus	hipopótamo (m)	[ipo'potamo]
kangaroo	canguro (m)	[kan'guro]
dog	perro (m)	['pero]

cow	vaca (f)	['baka]
bull	toro (m)	['toro]
sheep (ewe)	oveja (f)	[o'βeχa]
goat	cabra (f)	['kaβra]

donkey	asno (m)	['asno]
pig, hog	cerdo (m)	['θerðo]
hen (chicken)	gallina (f)	[ga'jina]
rooster	gallo (m)	['gajo]

duck	pato (m)	['pato]
goose	ganso (m)	['ganso]
turkey (hen)	pava (f)	['paβa]
sheepdog	perro (m) pastor	['pero pas'tor]

23. Animals. Part 2

bird	pájaro (m)	['paχaro]
pigeon	paloma (f)	[pa'loma]
sparrow	gorrión (m)	[gori'jon]
tit (great tit)	paro (m)	['paro]
magpie	cotorra (f)	[ko'tora]

eagle	águila (f)	['aɣilⁱa]
hawk	azor (m)	[a'θor]
falcon	halcón (m)	[alⁱ'kon]

swan	cisne (m)	['θisne]
crane	grulla (f)	['gruja]
stork	cigüeña (f)	[θiɣu'enja]
parrot	loro (m), papagayo (m)	['loro], [papa'ɣajo]
peacock	pavo (m) real	['paβo re'alⁱ]
ostrich	avestruz (m)	[aβes'truθ]

heron	garza (f)	['garθa]
nightingale	ruiseñor (m)	[ruise'njor]
swallow	golondrina (f)	[golon'drina]

woodpecker	pico (m)	['piko]
cuckoo	cuco (m)	['kuko]
owl	lechuza (f)	[le'tʃuθa]

penguin	pingüino (m)	[pingu'ino]
tuna	atún (m)	[a'tun]
trout	trucha (f)	['trutʃa]
eel	anguila (f)	[an'giⁱa]

shark	tiburón (m)	[tiβu'ron]
crab	centolla (f)	[θen'toja]
jellyfish	medusa (f)	[me'ðusa]
octopus	pulpo (m)	['pulʲpo]

starfish	estrella (f) de mar	[es'treja de mar]
sea urchin	erizo (m) de mar	[e'riθo de mar]
seahorse	caballito (m) de mar	[kaβa'jito de mar]
shrimp	camarón (m)	[kama'ron]

snake	serpiente (f)	[ser'pjente]
viper	víbora (f)	['biβora]
lizard	lagarto (f)	[lʲa'ɣarto]
iguana	iguana (f)	[iɣu'ana]
chameleon	camaleón (m)	[kamale'on]
scorpion	escorpión (m)	[eskorpi'on]

turtle	tortuga (f)	[tor'tuɣa]
frog	rana (f)	['rana]
crocodile	cocodrilo (m)	[koko'ðrilo]

insect, bug	insecto (m)	[in'sekto]
butterfly	mariposa (f)	[mari'posa]
ant	hormiga (f)	[or'miɣa]
fly	mosca (f)	['moska]

mosquito	mosquito (m)	[mos'kito]
beetle	escarabajo (m)	[eskara'βaχo]
bee	abeja (f)	[a'βeχa]
spider	araña (f)	[a'ranja]

24. Trees. Plants

tree	árbol (m)	['arβolʲ]
birch	abedul (m)	[aβe'ðulʲ]
oak	roble (m)	['roβle]
linden tree	tilo (m)	['tilo]
aspen	pobo (m)	['poβo]

| maple | arce (m) | ['arθe] |
| spruce | picea (m) | [pi'θea] |

pine	**pino** (m)	['pino]
cedar	**cedro** (m)	['θeðro]
poplar	**álamo** (m)	['alʲamo]
rowan	**serbal** (m)	[ser'βalʲ]
beech	**haya** (f)	['aja]
elm	**olmo** (m)	['olʲmo]
ash (tree)	**fresno** (m)	['fresno]
chestnut	**castaño** (m)	[kas'tanjo]
palm tree	**palmera** (f)	[palʲ'mera]
bush	**mata** (f)	['mata]
mushroom	**seta** (f)	['seta]
poisonous mushroom	**seta** (f) **venenosa**	['seta bene'nosa]
cep (Boletus edulis)	**seta calabaza** (f)	['seta kala'βaθa]
russula	**rúsula** (f)	['rusulʲa]
fly agaric	**matamoscas** (m)	[mata'moskas]
death cap	**oronja** (f) **verde**	[o'ronχa 'berðe]
flower	**flor** (f)	[flor]
bouquet (of flowers)	**ramo** (m) **de flores**	['ramo de 'flores]
rose (flower)	**rosa** (f)	['rosa]
tulip	**tulipán** (m)	[tuli'pan]
carnation	**clavel** (m)	[klʲa'βelʲ]
camomile	**manzanilla** (f)	[manθa'nija]
cactus	**cacto** (m)	['kakto]
lily of the valley	**muguete** (m)	[mu'ɣete]
snowdrop	**campanilla** **de las nieves**	[kampa'nija de lʲas 'njeβes]
water lily	**nenúfar** (m)	[ne'nufar]
greenhouse (tropical ~)	**invernadero** (m)	[imberna'ðero]
lawn	**césped** (m)	['θespeð]
flowerbed	**macizo** (m) **de flores**	[ma'θiθo de 'flores]
plant	**planta** (f)	['plʲanta]
grass	**hierba** (f)	['jerβa]
leaf	**hoja** (f)	['oχa]
petal	**pétalo** (m)	['petalo]
stem	**tallo** (m)	['tajo]
young plant (shoot)	**retoño** (m)	[re'tonjo]
cereal crops	**cereales** (m pl)	[θere'ales]
wheat	**trigo** (m)	['triɣo]
rye	**centeno** (m)	[θen'teno]
oats	**avena** (f)	[a'βena]
millet	**mijo** (m)	['miχo]
barley	**cebada** (f)	[θe'βaða]
corn	**maíz** (m)	[ma'iθ]
rice	**arroz** (m)	[a'roθ]

25. Various useful words

balance (of situation)	**balance** (m)	[ba'lʲanθe]
base (basis)	**base** (f)	['base]
beginning	**principio** (m)	[prin'θipjo]
category	**categoría** (f)	[kateɣo'ria]
choice	**elección** (f)	[elek'θjon]
coincidence	**coincidencia** (f)	[kojnθi'ðenθja]
comparison	**comparación** (f)	[kompara'θjon]
degree (extent, amount)	**grado** (m)	['graðo]
development	**desarrollo** (m)	[desa'rojo]
difference	**diferencia** (f)	[dife'renθja]
effect (e.g., of drugs)	**efecto** (m)	[e'fekto]
effort (exertion)	**esfuerzo** (m)	[esfu'erθo]
element	**elemento** (m)	[ele'mento]
example (illustration)	**ejemplo** (m)	[e'χemplo]
fact	**hecho** (m)	['etʃo]
help	**ayuda** (f)	[a'juða]
ideal	**ideal** (m)	[iðe'alʲ]
kind (sort, type)	**tipo** (m)	['tipo]
mistake, error	**error** (m)	[e'ror]
moment	**momento** (m)	[mo'mento]
obstacle	**obstáculo** (m)	[oβs'takulo]
part (~ of sth)	**parte** (f)	['parte]
pause (break)	**pausa** (f)	['pausa]
position	**posición** (f)	[posi'θjon]
problem	**problema** (m)	[pro'βlema]
process	**proceso** (m)	[pro'θeso]
progress	**progreso** (m)	[pro'ɣreso]
property (quality)	**propiedad** (f)	[propje'ðað]
reaction	**reacción** (f)	[reak'θjon]
risk	**riesgo** (m)	['rjesɣo]
secret	**secreto** (m)	[se'kreto]
series	**serie** (f)	['serje]
shape (outer form)	**forma** (f)	['forma]
situation	**situación** (f)	[situa'θjon]
solution	**solución** (f)	[solʲu'θjon]
standard (adj)	**estándar** (adj)	[es'tandar]
stop (pause)	**alto** (m)	['alʲto]
style	**estilo** (m)	[es'tilo]
system	**sistema** (m)	[sis'tema]

| table (chart) | **tabla** (f) | ['taβlʲa] |
| tempo, rate | **tempo** (m) | ['tempo] |

term (word, expression)	**término** (m)	['termino]
truth (e.g., moment of ~)	**verdad** (f)	[ber'ðað]
turn (please wait your ~)	**turno** (m)	['turno]
urgent (adj)	**urgente** (adj)	[ur'xente]

utility (usefulness)	**utilidad** (f)	[utili'ðað]
variant (alternative)	**variante** (f)	[ba'rjante]
way (means, method)	**modo** (m)	['moðo]
zone	**zona** (f)	['θona]

26. Modifiers. Adjectives. Part 1

additional (adj)	**adicional** (adj)	[aðiθjo'nalʲ]
ancient (~ civilization)	**antiguo** (adj)	[an'tiɣuo]
artificial (adj)	**artificial** (adj)	[artifi'θjalʲ]
bad (adj)	**malo** (adj)	['malo]
beautiful (person)	**bello** (adj)	['bejo]

big (in size)	**grande** (adj)	['grande]
bitter (taste)	**amargo** (adj)	[a'marɣo]
blind (sightless)	**ciego** (adj)	['θjeɣo]
central (adj)	**central** (adj)	[θen'tralʲ]

children's (adj)	**infantil** (adj)	[imfan'tilʲ]
clandestine (secret)	**clandestino** (adj)	[klʲandes'tino]
clean (free from dirt)	**limpio** (adj)	['limpjo]
clever (smart)	**inteligente** (adj)	[inteli'xente]
compatible (adj)	**compatible** (adj)	[kompa'tiβle]

contented (satisfied)	**contento** (adj)	[kon'tento]
dangerous (adj)	**peligroso** (adj)	[peli'ɣroso]
dead (not alive)	**muerto** (adj)	[mu'erto]
dense (fog, smoke)	**denso** (adj)	['denso]
difficult (decision)	**difícil** (adj)	[di'fiθilʲ]

dirty (not clean)	**sucio** (adj)	['suθjo]
easy (not difficult)	**fácil** (adj)	['faθilʲ]
empty (glass, room)	**vacío** (adj)	[ba'θio]
exact (amount)	**exacto** (adj)	[e'ksakto]
excellent (adj)	**excelente** (adj)	[ekθe'lente]

excessive (adj)	**excesivo** (adj)	[ekθe'siβo]
exterior (adj)	**exterior** (adj)	[ekste'rjor]
fast (quick)	**rápido** (adj)	['rapiðo]
fertile (land, soil)	**fértil** (adj)	['fertilʲ]
fragile (china, glass)	**frágil** (adj)	['fraxilʲ]
free (at no cost)	**gratis** (adj)	['gratis]

fresh (~ water)	**dulce** (adj)	['dulʲθe]
frozen (food)	**congelado** (adj)	[konχe'lʲaðo]
full (completely filled)	**lleno** (adj)	['jeno]
happy (adj)	**feliz** (adj)	[fe'liθ]
hard (not soft)	**duro** (adj)	['duro]
huge (adj)	**enorme** (adj)	[e'norme]
ill (sick, unwell)	**enfermo** (adj)	[eɱ'fermo]
immobile (adj)	**inmóvil** (adj)	[in'moβilʲ]
important (adj)	**importante** (adj)	[impor'tante]
interior (adj)	**interior** (adj)	[inte'rjor]
last (e.g., ~ week)	**último** (adj)	['ulʲtimo]
last (final)	**último** (adj)	['ulʲtimo]
left (e.g., ~ side)	**izquierdo** (adj)	[iθ'kjerðo]
legal (legitimate)	**legal** (adj)	[le'ɣalʲ]
light (in weight)	**ligero** (adj)	[li'χero]
liquid (fluid)	**líquido** (adj)	['likiðo]
long (e.g., ~ hair)	**largo** (adj)	['lʲarɣo]
loud (voice, etc.)	**fuerte** (adj)	[fu'erte]
low (voice)	**bajo** (adj)	['baχo]

27. Modifiers. Adjectives. Part 2

main (principal)	**principal** (adj)	[prinθi'palʲ]
matt, matte	**mate** (adj)	['mate]
mysterious (adj)	**misterioso** (adj)	[misteri'oso]
narrow (street, etc.)	**estrecho** (adj)	[es'tretʃo]
native (~ country)	**natal** (adj)	[na'talʲ]
negative (~ response)	**negativo** (adj)	[neɣa'tiβo]
new (adj)	**nuevo** (adj)	[nu'eβo]
next (e.g., ~ week)	**siguiente** (adj)	[si'ɣjente]
normal (adj)	**normal** (adj)	[nor'malʲ]
not difficult (adj)	**no difícil** (adj)	[no di'fiθilʲ]
obligatory (adj)	**obligatorio** (adj)	[oβliɣa'torjo]
old (house)	**viejo** (adj)	['bjeχo]
open (adj)	**abierto** (adj)	[a'βjerto]
opposite (adj)	**opuesto** (adj)	[opu'esto]
ordinary (usual)	**ordinario** (adj)	[orði'narjo]
original (unusual)	**original** (adj)	[oriχi'nalʲ]
polite (adj)	**cortés** (adj)	[kor'tes]
poor (not rich)	**pobre** (adj)	['poβre]
possible (adj)	**posible** (adj)	[po'siβle]
principal (main)	**principal** (adj)	[prinθi'palʲ]
probable (adj)	**probable** (adj)	[pro'βaβle]

prolonged (e.g., ~ applause)	continuo (adj)	[kon'tinuo]
public (open to all)	público (adj)	['puβliko]
rare (adj)	raro (adj)	['raro]
raw (uncooked)	crudo (adj)	['kruðo]
right (not left)	derecho (adj)	[de'retʃo]
ripe (fruit)	maduro (adj)	[ma'ðuro]
risky (adj)	arriesgado (adj)	[arjes'ɣaðo]
sad (~ look)	triste (adj)	['triste]
second hand (adj)	de segunda mano	[ðe se'ɣunda 'mano]
shallow (water)	poco profundo (adj)	['poko pro'fundo]
sharp (blade, etc.)	agudo (adj)	[a'ɣuðo]
short (in length)	corto (adj)	['korto]
similar (adj)	similar (adj)	[simi'lʲar]
small (in size)	pequeño (adj)	[pe'kenjo]
smooth (surface)	liso (adj)	['liso]
soft (~ toys)	blando (adj)	['blʲando]
solid (~ wall)	sólido (adj)	['soliðo]
sour (flavor, taste)	agrio (adj)	['aɣrjo]
spacious (house, etc.)	amplio (adj)	['ampljo]
special (adj)	especial (adj)	[espe'θjalʲ]
straight (line, road)	recto (adj)	['rekto]
strong (person)	fuerte (adj)	[fu'erte]
stupid (foolish)	tonto (adj)	['tonto]
superb, perfect (adj)	perfecto (adj)	[per'fekto]
sweet (sugary)	azucarado, dulce (adj)	[aθuka'raðo], ['dulʲθe]
tan (adj)	bronceado (adj)	[bronθe'aðo]
tasty (delicious)	sabroso (adj)	[sa'βroso]
unclear (adj)	poco claro (adj)	['poko 'klʲaro]

28. Verbs. Part 1

to accuse (vt)	acusar (vt)	[aku'sar]
to agree (say yes)	estar de acuerdo	[es'tar de aku'erðo]
to announce (vt)	anunciar (vt)	[anun'θjar]
to answer (vi, vt)	responder (vi, vt)	[respon'der]
to arrive (vi)	llegar (vi)	[je'ɣar]
to ask (~ oneself)	preguntar (vt)	[preɣun'tar]
to be absent	estar ausente	[es'tar au'sente]
to be afraid	tener miedo	[te'ner 'mjeðo]
to be born	nacer (vi)	[na'θer]
to be in a hurry	tener prisa	[te'ner 'prisa]
to beat (to hit)	pegar (vt)	[pe'ɣar]

to begin (vt)	comenzar (vi, vt)	[komen'θar]
to believe (in God)	creer (vi)	[kre'er]
to belong to …	pertenecer a …	[pertene'θer a]
to break (split into pieces)	quebrar (vt)	[ke'βrar]

to build (vt)	construir (vt)	[konstru'ir]
to buy (purchase)	comprar (vt)	[kom'prar]
can (v aux)	poder (v aux)	[po'ðer]
can (v aux)	poder (v aux)	[po'ðer]
to cancel (call off)	anular (vt)	[anuˈlʲar]

to catch (vt)	coger (vt)	[ko'χer]
to change (vt)	cambiar (vt)	[kam'bjar]
to check (to examine)	verificar (vt)	[berifi'kar]
to choose (select)	escoger (vt)	[esko'χer]
to clean up (tidy)	hacer la limpieza	[a'θer lʲa lim'pjeθa]

to close (vt)	cerrar (vt)	[θe'rar]
to compare (vt)	comparar (vt)	[kompa'rar]
to complain (vi, vt)	quejarse (vr)	[ke'χarse]
to confirm (vt)	confirmar (vt)	[komfir'mar]
to congratulate (vt)	felicitar (vt)	[feliθi'tar]
to cook (dinner)	preparar (vt)	[prepa'rar]
to copy (vt)	copiar (vt)	[ko'pjar]
to cost (vt)	costar (vt)	[kos'tar]
to count (add up)	contar (vt)	[kon'tar]
to count on …	contar con …	[kon'tar kon]

to create (vt)	crear (vt)	[kre'ar]
to cry (weep)	llorar (vi)	[jo'rar]
to dance (vi, vt)	bailar (vi, vt)	[bajˈlʲar]
to deceive (vi, vt)	engañar (vi, vt)	[enga'njar]
to decide (~ to do sth)	decidir (vt)	[deθi'ðir]

to delete (vt)	borrar (vt)	[bo'rar]
to demand (request firmly)	exigir (vt)	[eksi'χir]
to deny (vt)	negar (vt)	[ne'ɣar]
to depend on …	depender de …	[depen'der de]
to despise (vt)	despreciar (vt)	[despre'θjar]

to die (vi)	morir (vi)	[mo'rir]
to dig (vt)	cavar (vt)	[ka'βar]
to disappear (vi)	desaparecer (vi)	[desapare'θer]
to discuss (vt)	discutir (vt)	[disku'tir]
to disturb (vt)	molestar (vt)	[moles'tar]

29. Verbs. Part 2

| to dive (vi) | bucear (vi) | [buθe'ar] |
| to divorce (vi) | divorciarse (vr) | [diβor'θjarse] |

to do (vt)	**hacer** (vt)	[a'θer]
to doubt (have doubts)	**dudar** (vt)	[du'ðar]
to drink (vi, vt)	**beber** (vi, vt)	[be'βer]
to drop (let fall)	**dejar caer**	[de'χar ka'er]
to dry (clothes, hair)	**secar** (vt)	[se'kar]
to eat (vi, vt)	**comer** (vi, vt)	[ko'mer]
to end (~ a relationship)	**terminar** (vt)	[termi'nar]
to excuse (forgive)	**disculpar** (vt)	[diskuˡ'par]
to exist (vi)	**existir** (vi)	[eksis'tir]
to expect (foresee)	**prever** (vt)	[pre'βer]
to explain (vt)	**explicar** (vt)	[ekspli'kar]
to fall (vi)	**caer** (vi)	[ka'er]
to fight (street fight, etc.)	**pelear** (vi)	[pele'ar]
to find (vt)	**encontrar** (vt)	[eŋkon'trar]
to finish (vt)	**acabar, terminar** (vt)	[aka'βar], [termi'nar]
to fly (vi)	**volar** (vi)	[bo'lˡar]
to forbid (vt)	**prohibir** (vt)	[proi'βir]
to forget (vi, vt)	**olvidar** (vt)	[olˡβi'ðar]
to forgive (vt)	**perdonar** (vt)	[perðo'nar]
to get tired	**estar cansado**	[es'tar kan'saðo]
to give (vt)	**dar** (vt)	[dar]
to go (on foot)	**ir** (vi)	[ir]
to hate (vt)	**odiar** (vt)	[o'ðjar]
to have (vt)	**tener** (vt)	[te'ner]
to have breakfast	**desayunar** (vi)	[desaju'nar]
to have dinner	**cenar** (vi)	[θe'nar]
to have lunch	**almorzar** (vi)	[alˡmor'θar]
to hear (vt)	**oír** (vt)	[o'ir]
to help (vt)	**ayudar** (vt)	[aju'ðar]
to hide (vt)	**esconder** (vt)	[eskon'der]
to hope (vi, vt)	**esperar** (vi)	[espe'rar]
to hunt (vi, vt)	**cazar** (vi, vt)	[ka'θar]
to hurry (vi)	**tener prisa**	[te'ner 'prisa]
to insist (vi, vt)	**insistir** (vi)	[insis'tir]
to insult (vt)	**insultar** (vt)	[insulˡ'tar]
to invite (vt)	**invitar** (vt)	[imbi'tar]
to joke (vi)	**bromear** (vi)	[brome'ar]
to keep (vt)	**guardar** (vt)	[guar'ðar]
to kill (vt)	**matar** (vt)	[ma'tar]
to know (sb)	**conocer** (vt)	[kono'θer]
to know (sth)	**saber** (vt)	[sa'βer]
to like (I like …)	**gustar** (vi)	[gus'tar]
to look at …	**mirar a …**	[mi'rar a]
to lose (umbrella, etc.)	**perder** (vt)	[per'ðer]

to love (sb)	**querer, amar** (vt)	[ke'rer], [a'mar]
to make a mistake	**equivocarse** (vr)	[ekiβo'karse]
to meet (vi, vt)	**encontrarse** (vr)	[eŋkon'trarse]
to miss (school, etc.)	**faltar a …**	[falʲ'tar a]

30. Verbs. Part 3

to obey (vi, vt)	**obedecer** (vi, vt)	[oβeðe'θer]
to open (vt)	**abrir** (vt)	[a'βrir]
to participate (vi)	**participar** (vi)	[partiθi'par]
to pay (vi, vt)	**pagar** (vi, vt)	[pa'ɣar]
to permit (vt)	**permitir** (vt)	[permi'tir]

to play (children)	**jugar** (vi)	[χu'ɣar]
to pray (vi, vt)	**orar** (vi)	[o'rar]
to promise (vt)	**prometer** (vt)	[prome'ter]
to propose (vt)	**proponer** (vt)	[propo'ner]
to prove (vt)	**probar** (vt)	[pro'βar]
to read (vi, vt)	**leer** (vi, vt)	[le'er]

to receive (vt)	**recibir** (vt)	[reθi'βir]
to rent (sth from sb)	**alquilar** (vt)	[alʲki'lʲar]
to repeat (say again)	**repetir** (vt)	[repe'tir]
to reserve, to book	**reservar** (vt)	[reser'βar]
to run (vi)	**correr** (vi)	[ko'rer]

to save (rescue)	**salvar** (vt)	[salʲ'βar]
to say (~ thank you)	**decir** (vt)	[de'θir]
to see (vt)	**ver** (vt)	[ber]
to sell (vt)	**vender** (vt)	[ben'der]
to send (vt)	**enviar** (vt)	[em'bjar]
to shoot (vi)	**disparar, tirar** (vi)	[dispa'rar], [ti'rar]

to shout (vi)	**gritar** (vi)	[gri'tar]
to show (vt)	**mostrar** (vt)	[mos'trar]
to sign (document)	**firmar** (vt)	[fir'mar]
to sing (vi)	**cantar** (vi)	[kan'tar]
to sit down (vi)	**sentarse** (vr)	[sen'tarse]

to smile (vi)	**sonreír** (vi)	[sonre'ir]
to speak (vi, vt)	**hablar** (vi, vt)	[a'βlʲar]
to steal (money, etc.)	**robar** (vt)	[ro'βar]
to stop (please ~ calling me)	**cesar** (vt)	[θe'sar]
to study (vt)	**estudiar** (vt)	[estu'ðjar]

to swim (vi)	**nadar** (vi)	[na'ðar]
to take (vt)	**tomar** (vt)	[to'mar]
to talk to …	**hablar con …**	[a'βlʲar kon]
to tell (story, joke)	**contar** (vt)	[kon'tar]

to thank (vt)	**agradecer** (vt)	[aɣraðe'θer]
to think (vi, vt)	**pensar** (vi, vt)	[pen'sar]
to translate (vt)	**traducir** (vt)	[traðu'θir]
to trust (vt)	**confiar** (vt)	[koɱ'fjar]
to try (attempt)	**tratar de …**	[tra'tar de]
to turn (e.g., ~ left)	**girar** (vi)	[xi'rar]
to turn off	**apagar** (vt)	[apa'ɣar]
to turn on	**encender** (vt)	[enθen'der]
to understand (vt)	**comprender** (vt)	[kompren'der]
to wait (vt)	**esperar** (vt)	[espe'rar]
to want (wish, desire)	**querer** (vt)	[ke'rer]
to work (vi)	**trabajar** (vi)	[traβa'xar]
to write (vt)	**escribir** (vt)	[eskri'βir]

www.ingramcontent.com/pod-product-compliance
Lightning Source LLC
Chambersburg PA
CBHW070115070426
42448CB00039B/2877